Revisiting the Garden

Revisiting the Garden

AND DECIDING TO STAY

Dana J. Voght

All scripture quotations are taken from the HOLY BIBLE NEW INTERNATIONAL VERSION (R). NIV (R). Copyright (c) 1973, 1978, 1984 by International Bible Society. Used by permission of Zondervan Publishing House. All rights reserved.

Unless permission has been otherwise given, the names and identifying characteristics of the persons whose case histories are used in this book have been changed to preserve their privacy.

Cover picture: Mystic Journey; Copyright (c) 2001 by Marilyn Blessing.

Technical assistant for cover: Susan Ruda.

Photograph of the author by Lifetouch Portrait Studios, Inc.

This book was printed in the United States of America.

To order additional copies of this book, contact:
Xlibris Corporation
1-888-7-XLIBRIS
www.Xlibris.com
Orders@Xlibris.com

Contents

*This book is lovingly dedicated
to
Geoffrey M. Voght, my son
and to
Wendie J. Lombardi, my daughter.*

They are my joy forever.

Acknowledgements

Preparation for writing *Revisiting the Garden and Deciding to Stay* has taken over seventy-five years. Now while I contemplate my "Acknowledgements," certain individuals from those years come alive in my mind. I gratefully and lovingly acknowledge them as having been sacred Lights in my life which, otherwise, would have remained conflicted and stormy.

How is it that these shining souls came to me one by one during critical moments and contributed to my sacred self-discovery? How is it that they cared enough to walk awhile with me, each clearing away a portion of the jumbled, self-defeating concepts with which I was living? Surely the answer to this mystery can only be that the One Great Creative Spirit responded to my deeply felt, unarticulated soul cries. For all of them, I am truly grateful.

There was Lodema Cory, a minister's wife who made my teen-age years bearable, instructing me in "elocution" and encouraging my all-consuming interest and talent in the theatre. I have forgotten the full name of Dr. Sanders, my psychiatrist in Rochester, New York at the time of my decision to leave my abusive husband. In my mind's eye, I still relive the comforting memory of a session with Dr. Sanders. His undivided attention—punctuated for an instant by his tear-blurred eyes—assured me that he totally accepted me, valued my love of Jesus and approved of my reliance on Spirit. He lifted me from an emotional breakdown and reminded me that my two children were worth my staying alive. Today, I wonder how I could ever have considered suicide.

Vi and Albert Waeffler, my employers at the Lantana Palms Restaurant, were extraordinarily generous and protective of me and my two children when, in 1954, we first arrived in Florida and while I was obtaining a divorce. Rev. Mary Kupferle, my first Unity minister, introduced me to the Truth teachings of Charles and Myrtle Fillmore. For Mary and for the good people of Unity of Delray Beach, who prayerfully and financially supported my decision in 1972 to become a Unity minister, I am grateful.

I was, indeed, blessed when I met Akhter Ahsen, Ph.D. who taught me Eidetic Therapy and whose insight and guidance were and still are a God-send. Richard J. Santo, D.C., is a natural healer. He beheld the Spirit of Jesus in my soul and became a beloved friend with whom I can comfortably express my passion for Truth. His faith in my aspirations and his enthusiasm for *Revisiting the Garden and Deciding to Stay* have kept me centered whenever I have felt somewhat overwhelmed.

The reader/advisors of *Revisiting the Garden* are and will remain my cherished friends with whom I share this great quest for Love and Truth.

Not only have I been blessed by individuals that I have known personally. There have been the poets, authors, artists and musicians who have filled my heart to overflowing as only true artists can. The written teachings of Charles and Myrtle Fillmore, co-founders of Unity School of Christianity, are not only timeless; they are exacting and a stumbling block to those who are not wholehearted in their dedication. Many of Charles Fillmore's words are quoted in *Revisiting the Garden*.

I gratefully remember and cherish my hundreds of Eidetic students. They have referred others to me and have opened doors for my talks and seminars. Furthermore, we have grown in Spirit together. Most especially I thank those students who share their case histories in this book. What more proof of their spiritual growth through Eidetics is necessary? As their past and present pain was lifted, these folks became compassionate and wise. Today, without a second thought, they spontaneously guide others to the Garden of Truth and Love where Spirit dwells. By sharing their stories in this book, they contribute to the healing of the world. During this millennium the Cosmic Christ is, indeed, being lifted from the cross built by human consciousness.

The good people working behind the Reference Desk in the Blake Library located in Stuart, Florida have saved me many, many hours of research: tracking down present copyright owners and their addresses, researching dates, verifying authors and finding the exact wording of quotations, among other data. I am grateful for them. I also thank the folks in the Barnes and Nobel Cafe located in Jensen Beach, Florida for their relaxed atmosphere and their acceptance of the hours I have spent at one of their

tables, sipping coffee, clarifying my words and pen-
ning my thoughts on my yellow writing pad.

In God's Truth, everything is serendipitous.

Preface

When I began my work as a Unity minister, I found myself and some members of my congregation yearning to more truly live the teachings of Jesus, rather than just studying and trying to understand them. I also found that this yearning to experience the kind of life exemplified by avatars or holy men was shining in the hearts of loyal followers of faiths other than Christianity. The prevalent attitude of most people seemed to be that such a goal was impossible. One only did one's best and let it go at that. However, others who were challenged with compulsive and damaging behavior not only yearned for, they *needed* a fresh religious approach in order to overcome undesirable habits. There seemed to be a connection missing, a bridge between everyday life and the altruistic truths I taught from the pulpit. This was so obvious in counseling sessions that I became determined to find an answer.

While searching, I was introduced to Akhter

Ahsen, Ph.D., Founder of The Institute of Eidetic Therapy in Yonkers, New York. The result of this meeting is detailed as the case history in Chapter 1. Working with the student in that case opened my eyes as to how available Spirit is to each one of us, how active Spirit can be among us and how unaware and spiritually ignorant we are. Myself included. While studying under Dr. Ahsen I became an Eidetic Psychotherapist and explored the depths of the eidetic process. Surrounded by this Life Essence, the Eidos, I found the Spirit of God to be the bridge for which I was looking.

During more than eighteen years of spiritual counseling, I have used what I learned from Dr. Ahsen, stepping off from his use of Greek and Hindu mythology into Christian symbolism and images. The visions given to my students and me in Eidetics are as directive and meaningful as the visions received in Old and New Testament times. They give clear, sacred guidance to anyone wanting it, whether for making common, everyday decisions or for the healing of a conflicted soul. The participant receives a visual symbolic message from his/her *own* inner Spirit. That is to say, the message received has meaning only for that particular individual. Furthermore, Spirit opens the way for the eidetic student's realization of dreams, goals and a life filled with soul satisfaction.

The purpose of this book is to awaken the spiritually hungry reader—regardless of faith or human condition—to the moment by moment movement of Spirit in his/her consciousness, relationships and life. The everyday focus we have determines the quality of our own life and influences the lives of our neighbors, the development of our culture and even the relationships between nations.

People ask me what Eidetic Therapy is. Well, the word eidetic, can be defined as a memory involving accurate, vivid recall in visual images. The word is pronounced eye-DET-ic and derives from two Greek words: eidos, meaning "form," and idein, meaning "to see." Therefore, eidetic means to see form. But when used as a noun with a capital E, I find that an Eidetic is a transforming spiritual *experience* rather than just seeing a form. It is the experience, not a mere definition of Eidetics that reveals its nature and purpose.

Eidetics as I teach it involves the activity of Spirit in myself as well as in my students. During a session, I am in a meditative state, watching my student in the eidetic experience. God's Spirit moves through me offering silent encouragement and occasional verbal guidance. The purpose of the session is two-fold. First, Eidetics presents the student with his own God given solutions to perplexing questions and con-flicted relationships. Second, through spontaneous, symbolic, often humorous visionary experiences, Eidetics overcomes the student's painful life situa-tions by transforming his consciousness and his outer circumstances. I refer to my counselees as students because they learn to use the process for themselves. Going to the therapist for unending sessions is not necessary.

Dr. Ahsen describes the Eidetic as "a psychical visual image of unusual vividness. When this image is experienced in the mind, it is 'seen' clearly like a movie image. This inner 'seeing' is accompanied by pressure in the visual apparatus and a definite change in consciousness.

"The eidetic image," he continues, "has the qual-ity of remaining very constant, so that there is a long-term access to an important experience. The individual, being more open in this state, readily learns new emotional perspectives."(1)

The word, eidetic, has been used in psychological and philosophical circles for thousands of years, as it still is today. Our western scientific society has frowned on visions as being useless figments of the imagination. Only now are we awakening to the symbolic Truths found in certain forms of spontaneous imagery. Renewed spiritual interest in our country is cultivating an appreciation for the use of visions. There are those in our society, today, who are ready soil for the spiritual experiences that Eidetics offers Christianity and all faiths.

I trust that through contemplating the messages in the case histories and through the practice of the spiritual meditations in this book, the reader's awareness will be aroused. He will come to understand more about Eidetics and will experience the movement of Spirit in his mind and heart to a greater extent than before.

Because I am a devoted follower of Jesus Christ, my orientation is Christian. Through many mystical experiences, I have become what I am today. Jesus has responded to my cry during times of desperation and to my gratitude during times of joy. During His visitations with me, sometimes, His mystical form has been visible to my human eye. At other times His palpable Presence by my right shoulder is perceived in my spiritual eye. He is always available whether I am alone or in a room crowded with people. He is my Beloved Friend.

This precious intimate relationship is the most powerful, most influential aspect of my life. Love and Truth in my heart, though strong, are like fine, clear crystal that many have tried to shatter with intellectual analysis, criticism, ridicule and attempts to humiliate. Yet with each confrontation, I have ascended more into the realm of existence where God is creating me, Jesus is my constant Friend and Spirit is active through it all. But why differentiate into three, that which is One? God or Jesus or Spirit by any other name is God or Jesus or Spirit.

I learned early to remain silent, to tell no one about my spiritual experiences and convictions. God reveals Truth to everyone when he/she is open to learn. I thank Goodness that, today, spiritually advanced persons are appearing in my life one by one. They have no ego-need to crucify the Christ in me, and my heart sings its appreciation. These friends of mine and I share spiritual experiences and insight. Furthermore, we really listen to each other, because we believe.

For many reasons my teachings apply to *all* who seek to follow Truth. Christians often see Truth in other religions, especially those originating in the East. When someone is God-oriented, he is in tune with the Truth of Christ, although he might call this sacred Truth by another name. I am convinced that if such a person has not met Jesus as yet, he will recognize Him when he does.

Dr. Ahsen has an ongoing mythic relationship with Jesus Christ. Knowledgeable in eastern and western science, philosophy, mythology and psychology, he specializes in all areas of Eidetic Therapy, healing his patients' souls as well as their bodies. In November 2000, he received a citation from the Indian Council of Social Science Research in New Delhi. Besides his development of Image Psychology, a few of his accomplishments are his contributions to the cause of a "Peace Psychology," to non-violent resolution of conflict and to strengthening feminist perspectives on peacemaking. Dr. Ahsen moves in Spirit with the comprehension of a scholar who experiences his knowledge.

By opening the psyche to the sacred activity of the third eye, the eidetic student advances her desire and facilitates her ability to become One with God. Here—perceiving with the spiritual eye—the individual abides in the Life Essence of his being, sees as the Creator sees and finds that, indeed, all things are possible. Here, there is no time or space and both soul and body become whole. Here is a new dimension of being where hierarchy diminishes, where all issues of relationship and all levels of consciousness become one issue and one level. Here "many who are first will be last, and many who are last will be first" (Matthew 19:30). Here it is that God and man/woman are One, and that "doing" is effortless. In other words, the process described in this book shows a way to Oneness with Spirit as we revisit the Garden and enter the Kingdom of Heaven on earth.

My own focus is on becoming aware of, experiencing and facilitating the movement of God's Spirit in my life and in the lives of individuals whom I know. To cope with the rapid progression of our intellectual accomplishments in science and technology, we need finer, more altruistic motives than we have ever known. Spirit can give us this motivation through Truth and Love. For whatever God accomplishes through me in this respect, I am grateful. (See Epilogue, written after Septemeber 11, 2001.)

Most of the images and exercises in this book are those that have been developed at Centre. The words and terms I use have come naturally from my Christian beliefs and meditations, from my work with Dr. Ahsen, from healings I have received through conversations with Richard J. Santo, D.C., Natural Healer, and from sessions with my students. When I have used an exercise or illustration from Dr. Ahsen's book, *Psycheye*, or from one of my other mentor's work, I have so stated in my text.

Occasionally, I counsel someone from another faith or someone who calls himself an agnostic or atheist. An Eidetic Therapist can easily adapt the process to appropriate terminology for any student who is interested in loving, honoring and becoming One with Truth and Goodness. God, worshipped in Spirit and in Truth by any other name, is God.

During my individual sessions under Dr. Ahsen, I developed a caring relationship with the gods of Viking, Greek and Hindu mythology that included a Semitic connection. There is ironic humor and tremendous joy in turning cartwheels with Ganesh when surrounded by chaos. And I delight in the Celtic wisdom of John O'Donohue. By reminding me of my "clay" beginnings, he connects me with my earthiness as well as with my Divinity. Spirit is eternally active: Alpha and Omega!

Incidentally, some folks find the word, God, difficult to use because of their childhood exposure to teachings of a vengeful, unloving god. When one woman was a little girl, she hid, terrified, under a pew during church services so that God and Jesus couldn't get her. While you read this book, dear Friend, if the name God doesn't sit well on your mind and heart, be assured that your Creator, the Most Ancient Consciousness, understands. Please substitute another word for God. There are many: Spirit,

Allah, Lord, Jehovah, Shiva, Krishna and Buddha, to name a few. In Truth these words are One and the same.

It is vital to the melding of our diversified cultural beliefs and to our expansive global society that we not allow foreign sounding words, accents and unfamiliar expressions to confuse and separate us. We must learn to love one another beyond words that tend to turn us off from Truth.

My students and I have found certain words and terms to be meaningful in our eidetic studies. There follows a list of some of these expressions and their significance as I use them in this book:

Centre: my room, sacred space for counseling.

clay beginnings: " . . . the Lord God formed the man from the dust of the ground . . ." (Genesis 2:7).

Eidetic, Eidetic Therapy: the process developed by Dr. Ahsen; an activity experienced in the Life Essence and perceived with the single eye.

eidetic: the adjective.

eidetic: the use as a common noun, refers to the general process of mentally seeing form.

eidetic experience: the state of being so involved in a vision that one feels it physically and psychologically, as though it were an actual present occurrence.

fact: the human perception of the way things are.

Father-Mother-Creator: Father signifies Principle, the masculine, thinking aspect of God; Mother signifies Love, the feminine, feeling aspect of God.

he, she, his, hers: are used interchangeably.

Life Essence: the deepest consciousness or the Christ consciousness where one sees with the spiritual eye, where there is neither time nor space, and where divine healing and sacred guidance take place.

Most Ancient or Most Ancient One: Our Creator; the Omnipotent, Omnipresent, Omniscient First Cause; the Lord of all.

student: my counselees are students because they learn the eidetic process for themselves so that it is beneficial to them during their entire lives. Through Eidetics they learn to rely on Spirit.

Truth: God's perception of the way things are.

unconscious, nonconscious: lack of an awareness of the Spiritual.

Truth longs to take possession of your mind, soul and body. It is my passion to influence others to awaken to Spirit, so that they invite the movement of Spirit to take over the moment by moment activity of their lives. In the *nature* of Jesus, everyone can become One with Spirit. "I and the Father are One" (John 10:30).

My helpful reader/advisors, after they read my first drafts, suggested that I share the details of one or two case studies with you. I do this in Chapters 1, 6 and 7 of *Revisiting the Garden and Deciding to Stay.* They wanted more exposure to and understanding of how my eidetic students evolve. In chapters 2 through 5 and 8 through 10, spiritual insights are shared, insights that I received during therapy sessions with students and during my private moments of meditation. Throughout this book fictitious names have been used unless individual permission has been received to use real names.

At the end of each chapter there is at least one meditation. I suggest that you, dear Reader, use each of them as directed and practice those that are the

most meaningful. One or two are repeated and expanded from chapter to chapter. It is important also
for you to experience and to work with your own
sacred visions. If you ask for them, they will be given
to you.

What My Reader/ Advisors Are Saying

Rev. Dana J. Voght's insight into the soul needs of her students expands to include national and global needs for healing. Through case studies, meditations and spiritual wisdom, *Revisiting the Garden and Deciding to Stay* leads the reader along a sacred path. He/She learns to recognize and accept the mysterious, always beneficial activity of Spirit.

So far reaching is this hallowed activity that through the technique Rev. Voght offers, Spirit transforms much more than one individual person. During this millennium, as we accept the moment by moment activity of God's Spirit, the chaos experienced by the world's people is being replaced with Love, Peace and Divine Order.

Rev. Ernestine Griffin, Founder-Minister
Unity on Campus Ministry
University of Michigan in Ann Arbor

Dana Voght immediately piques curiosity with an account of a counseling session, and then captures attention as she recounts her eventually successful search for a modality which will help her client. The meditations at the end of chapters draw the reader into the eidetic process which Dana has practiced for eighteen years. They make the book an interactive experience for the reader and a valuable spiritually based self-help tool.

Rev. Hypatia Hasbrouck (1921-2001)
Author of
Handbook of Positive Prayer
Red Riding Hood in Jerusalem
The Trip to Bethlehem

Dana draws from a deep spiritual well within herself, bringing forth Truth in a gentle, powerful way! She weaves her spirituality, philosophy, and experiences into an interesting and poignant narrative—sure to enrich the lives of all who read her book.

Some books are wordy, wasting our time in "getting to the point." Dana wastes no words! She clearly and concisely presents her ideas—"seed ideas" that will germinate within our consciousness.

Rev. Marilyn Rieger, Co-Minister
Unity of Vero Beach
Vero Beach, Florida

Read this book to find the path to expressing your Life to its full potential, replacing fear and doubt with Faith and Confidence.

Richard J. Santo, D.C.
134 Bridge Road
Tequesta, Florida 33469

Introduction

LIFE AND DEATH SAINTS

By Akhter Ahsen, Ph.D.

For a moment I try to imagine in my mind the ancient Temple of Delphi where the original inscription at the entrance read: "Know Thyself." Instead of imagining that particular temple, my mind imagines another one in the same spot which looks somewhat similar from the outside, but on the entrance of the building the inscription is different. It reads, "Life and Death Saints."

What is this mysterious intermingling of messages all about? I am being informed that there are people who are born in this world as saints, but the world has never known them or recognized them as such. As children they were never given a nod of approval but instead were told what was wrong with them. They were spiritual children and since they were not born into an established order of priesthood, they were discarded and cruelly thrown away. Another vision was imposed on them instead. Their true face became concealed behind a mysterious veil.

These individuals have the fullest life in them, but they have suffered the worst persecution, being light bearers in the dark corridors of history as the "Life and Death Saints." In them, life and death are interwoven into the mysterious fabric of a veil which needs to be penetrated. Deep down they know everything that life represents—but neurosis, anxiety, depression, confusion and a lack of personal identity have been their daily bread. They cannot be known unless someone else really comes forward, senses their true identity and affirms it. Then they can be set free on their journey.

Someone may, in fact, come forward and affirm the true saintliness of these "life and death" individuals, but strange as it may seem there is yet another hurdle to be crossed before they can be fulfilled. Paradoxically, as the second step, they need to be affirmed by themselves. This final self-realization is the true revelation of their self-identity and the lifting of the veil which has covered their truth for so long. One can call this fulfilling experience by the various names which are customarily given to the healing process, but truly a surprising event has occurred. Not only has a profound healing taken place, but a true healer has come forward from behind the mysterious veil. This leads to the third step: These individuals must go out into the world and save others in a similar way. The confusion about self-identity has been turned around into a miracle through this self-discovery. But there really is no mystery here to speak of. The person was a healer to begin with and it took an intuitive outsider, like a water diviner, to locate the miracle maker. As a result, alienation was replaced by a feeling of inner discovery and unity. Who are you, or who am I is a fundamental question regarding this meta-unity between the knower and the known.

I once asked the same question of a woman from California who was in therapy with me. Her sole quest in life had been this trying to find her true identity. She informed me that over the past many years a dark veil had descended over her, and now the veil was so thick and so dark that she could not see the outside world or make contact with it. She answered the next question which I proceeded to ask of her: whether or not she had ever felt when she was a child that deep down somewhere she was really a saint. She related this rather significant incident around her First Communion.

"As a child I did not know what sin was. How could I? I did not know if I was doing everything right. There was always discomfort and fear. My First Communion was a strange event. I confessed my sins and left, although the priest had not yet opened the door. I was told that I should have waited for the opening of the door. So, I took the host without the proper confession."

She was asked to remember herself in the past as a child and a saint. Recalling her father's opinion in this respect, she said, "I think my father saw saintliness in me. My mother would have a fit of jealousy over it when he discussed such things with me. At age 6, I had a conflict with my mother over something, and my mother said that I was lying. My father intervened and said, 'No, she does not lie.'"

At this point she was asked to see an image of

herself as a saint, and she produced a particularly strong image: an eidetic one. She said, "A rose comes to my mind, and the rose is on top of a book, a leather bound book." This image became the beginning point of discovery regarding her true identity that deep down there was a saintly side to her, that it needed to be recognized by someone, and that in the end she also needed to recognize it herself.

According to the story which has come down to us about the Crucifixion, Jesus was put on the cross and when he thirsted for water, gall was given to him instead. Traditionally, in most cultures, including some of those connected with the Old Testament, people give honey to babies when they are born. The honey is not only a sweet welcome, but also a rebirth image, because the child is going to face the excruciating pain of the world later on in life.

During one of the many mythic journeys I have taken in my mind, I once decided to break in my own mind the relentless symbolism of pain on the cross, and I used the image of honey. In the image, Jesus thirsted at the cross and gall was offered to him as a nasty and cruel gesture. I went over to the cross, recognized the pain and with utter love and adoration offered Jesus honey. I was surprised to see that in the image people began to quarrel with me. But I felt some spontaneous courage and I shouted back at them. At that moment I thought of the baby Jesus who was given honey at birth, and I saw that by offering honey to Jesus on the cross I was welcoming him into the world. The hostile crowd dispersed and the vision ended at this point.

When I was reading Rev. Dana J. Voght's book I had the feeling that she was offering the same mythical honey to the readers. Page after page I heard this nectar-like refrain in her song of transformations as the main theme: The lofty vision of human reality is God's own true reality. The invitation was to align with the plan of One who is this universe and who knows all that is in the universe and is not separate from the universe. One must overcome all the divisions. Over the years when I developed the eidetic method which Rev. Voght has so ably discussed in this book, the aim was the same: to find a method which overcomes all those divisions that split the foundations of the mind. I believe that this book effectively presents the eidetic method through a language that holds the mystique of the image in a loving embrace.

The therapist or the healer has to remove the historically irritating material as a preliminary measure, so that the saintly person on the other side can be clearly seen. After the gall of history has been recognized and removed, love must come forward. In this, the eidetic imagery serves as a unifying instrument of inquiry and healing.

In my own life I became aware of this hidden mystery which I find as the final message at the Temple of Delphi where the inscription "Life and Death Saints" super-imposed itself over "Know Thyself." In this Temple Jesus himself became the final illumination. The mystery is all about the love that has been forgotten and put away. People have to be loved by someone before they can love themselves. For the discovery of true saintliness, sainthood and saving of the world, the dictum for me or, for that matter, any other person has to be:

"*I have to love them before they can love themselves.*"

This is the true mission of a true healer, the one who truly brings other healers forward.

Akhter Ahsen, Ph.D.

Image Institute
22 Edgecliff Terrace
Yonkers, New York 10705

INDIAN COUNCIL OF SOCIAL SCIENCE RESEARCH

CITATION OF HONOUR

PROFESSOR AKHTER AHSEN (b. 6 February 1933) Fellow of the American Psychological Association and the American Psychological Society, New York, U.S.A. is a renowned scholar of the South Asian Region. He has made pioneering contribution to psychological science. He has made immense contribution in the field of Image Psychology. The thrust of the imagery movement as follows Ahsen's lead, is that the image is the most central to human activity and expression much as behaviourists believe that behaviour is central.

Image Psychology, as propounded by Professor Ahsen, represents an experiential system of complex mental structures and dynamic image formation that demonstrate various functions and operations of the mind and body. It discovers imaginary blueprints in the psyche, locates them at their source and traces their tributory.

Its theory accounts for both eastern and western traditions of science and philosophy as is shown in his latest books Hot and Cold: Mental Imagery-Mind Over Body and Encounters. Besides his contribution to the field of image psychology Professor Ahsen has authored many literary works notable among them are his epic poem 'Manhunt in the Desert'. In this book Professor Ahsen, brings us through many crises of illusory findings, mirages and then again only rock and sand, finally to the end of the road, which is where the water is . . . , remarked Joseph Campbell. Professor Ahsen's psychological concepts and researches have contributed to the development of a dynamic "Peace Psychology" and critical thinking for non-violent resolution of conflict, and the promotion of tolerance for plurality of viewpoints. He has also contributed to strengthening feminist perspectives on peace making. He has established the psychological principles of a new movement for moral, spiritual and intellectual transformation of the Third Millenium to overcome the clash of civilisation.

In horouring him in the year of the fifty-third anniversary of India's independence, the Indian Council of Social Science Research acknowledges him a true friend of India, and a living treasure of the South Asian Cultural Community:

November 2000

Professor M.L.Sandhi
Chairman
ICSSR, New Delhi

PROLOGUE

This time
The Book shall be written,
On the vast pages
Of the Desert itself.

It will not be written
On the barks of trees,
Nor on the skins of animals,
Nor on paper.

Trees are gone,
Animals are hidden,
And the paper is dirty and filthy.
So, he will write
On the pages of the Desert itself.

The tradition of teaching
By word of mouth is over.
This time He will teach not orally
But physically.
This time He will not offer
Words or symbols in place of Man,
But Man himself.
This time
The Book shall be written
On the body of Man. (1)

Akhter Ahsen, Ph.D.
Manhunt In The Desert, page 3

Chapter 1

THE MOVEMENT OF SPIRIT

*Call to me and I will answer you and tell you
great and unsearchable things you do not know.*
Jeremiah 33:3

A handsome, young, university art student lay on
my office couch. He preferred that to sitting in
a chair, because he often felt dizzy and nauseated
during counseling. His body bore scars from beatings and from a gunshot wound, evidence of childhood abuse inflicted by his mother.

His religious background was literal and strict.
Thus, his family and friends looked askance at him
and his fiancée when they started attending the
church where I served as an ordained New Thought
minister. Worse, during the seventies and eighties,
many in that section of the South shunned any

woman minister—and I was the first in the city—as being possessed by the devil. Nevertheless, I wanted to help this troubled youth.

"It's so hard," Greg finally told me, "to tell my minister that I hate my mother. I fantasize getting even with her. Then I feel guilty. I'm supposed to forgive her, but I've tried, and I just can't."

He often exploded in a rage, using abusive language toward friends and relatives and, also, toward co-workers, making it impossible to keep a job very long. During his weekly counseling, he started denying the power of anything or anyone to keep his healing from him and, in a lovely poetic style, he wrote his own affirmations. He practiced exercises of forgiveness, and we prayed together for his increased compassion and understanding. When each session ended, Greg felt renewed peace and freedom, but his God-centered ability to face life with wholesome, nonviolent responses did not last.

Toward the end of one session, he sat with his head in his hands and tears in his eyes. "How can I marry the girl I love unless I overcome my anger?" he asked. "What guarantee does she have that I won't lose my temper and become violent with her and our children?"

Perhaps, I thought, one of the psychological methods, used in addition to spiritual counseling, held the cure we were seeking. I considered Transactional Analysis, Neurolinguistics, dream analysis and group therapy. Most secular techniques serve constructive purposes, but none of these alternatives appealed to Greg. Being of an artistic nature and a man who held his own counsel, he preferred a one-on-one spiritual approach.

He left our meetings with an increase in the self-esteem for which he yearned. However, Greg was like the man who diligently used his denials and affirmations and then told his minister, "Oh, I still have the same old problems, but on a much higher level." His intellectual grasp of principle was flawless. After each session he'd be fine for a few hours or days. Then, with no warning, uncontrollable fury would erupt again creating the same old problems. His fear that his verbal abuse would become physical persisted.

God is in every situation. Light is in every darkness. Victory is in every challenge. Despite our frustration, the search for a spiritual means of healing his emotions continued.

Little by little, Greg revealed details of his childhood. He was the eldest of two boys, the only living children in his family. The beatings that had been inflicted on him by his mother were ignored by his father, and his younger brother suffered none of the mistreatment.

Eventually a memory surfaced. When Greg was a toddler, he had an older brother with whom he was playing ball in the front yard. His mother sat nearby on the porch, chatting with a friend. Greg threw the ball into the street. His brother chased it into the path of a car that killed him. The distraught mother blamed Greg. He attempted to escape her repeated assaults by retreating behind the closed door of his small bedroom. There he created his own world, writing poetry and drawing pictures of grand adventures that he experienced in his mind. His family regarded him as a daydreamer and belittled his artistic abilities.

During counseling, he developed an understanding of the destructive dynamics within his family, but

the persistent pain imbedded in his memory continued to undermine his self-esteem. His willingness to
confront and to work through the torment in his
soul and, thereby, to become a wholesome human
being was heart wrenching to witness.

We had no intention of terminating our search
until God's direction for us was found. The ancient
promise in Jeremiah 29:13 is, "You will seek me and
find me when you seek me with all your heart." We
made a specific request, asking God for a spiritual
bridge that would span the gap between Greg's practical, everyday living and the Principles I taught from
the pulpit. Then we received our answer.

One day, over lunch, I told a psychiatrist from my
congregation of my dilemma. I asked if he knew of
any healing therapy that I could use along with the
spiritual principles taught by Jesus.

He certainly did. The doctor introduced me to
Akhter Ahsen, Ph. D., a man from Pakistan, who had
researched imagery and established the Institute of
Eidetic Imagery in Yonkers, New York. His teachings
give the student a spiritual approach that enables
him/her to move beyond mind-body-soul separation
and into the essential unity that is the individual self
as a divine human being.

While training under Dr. Ahsen, I adapted his
eidetic use of eastern religious symbolism to the
Christian experience. Later, with some of my students,
I started using non-Christian terminology to communicate with universal Spirit. Most importantly from
the beginning, Greg responded to the process and
his healing began.

It is possible for an individual to experience spontaneous—rather than intellectually determined—
images of life situations in a way that heals unpleas-

ant memories and carries each one along a sacred passage to his/her more fulfilling life. Like visions received in Biblical times, this technique functions as a guide, a catalyst for new perception and new emotional responses resulting in a definite growth in consciousness.

Such healing can be likened to Kirlian photography, in which the energy of a broken leaf appears, making the picture of the leaf whole and complete. Just so, as Eidetics heals the pain of the mutilated soul, it frees captive underlying energies and the wholesome person appears eager to experience a higher order of living.

Anyone using this powerful process finds that relationships are healed without a word being spoken. Reconciliations occur in all areas of life: between our rational mind and our emotions and in our personal surrounding world. The healing and the transformation take place in the Life Essence of one's being. There, Spirit remains uncaged and moves freely. Carried on the wings of the deeply felt spiritual experience, Spirit easily and effectively reaches and reveals the Essence of others in the relationship. Balance and harmony are established between one's thinking and feeling natures. Body, mind and Spirit unite in the birth of the authentic Self as we reclaim our Oneness with God. We must remember this: Our true identity is as God images us. Our true parent is our Father-Mother-Creator. Our biological parents are just that—we came through them for this lifetime; that is all.

This movement of Spirit carried Greg from one sequential quest to another. One day, he acknowledged, "I've got to tell you. I keep having this terrible dream that I kill my mother. It's such a relief when I wake up. I know I'm not going to kill her, but I want to."

Intentionally stepping off from this nightmare, an eidetic vision formed. Greg experienced himself as the little boy, enduring one of his mother's beatings. Although his pleas to her and his weak attempts to stop her failed, suddenly he informed me, "Well, I don't know where that came from! A voice just said to me, 'Every mother loves her baby.' I'll never believe that!"

But eidetic visions do not lie, and we decided to remember the message. Nevertheless, he still could not look into his mother's eyes in the spiritual experience and forgive her.

This counseling occurred during the 1980s. Greg and his college friends were interested in the King Arthur legends. Groups dressed up as knights and battled evil with fancy, imitation swords and other weapons. The activity of creating his own costume and the pretense of aggressive outer behavior appealed to Greg's artistic, troubled soul. The theme worked well in Eidetics, also. During one session, he confronted a gargoyle in a dark cave. The creature, dripping blood, reached out with bone-like fingers, attempting to kill him. In the terrifying reality of the vision, Greg spoke aloud, "What'll I do?"

He implored the Universe for a symbolic tool with which to protect himself. Grabbing an offered sword he threw it toward the gargoyle. But he said, "I don't want to kill it; just to scare it away." The gargoyle grasped the sword and thrust it into itself, crying:

"The sword is yours to bear at will.
Your words are strength;
Your dreams, your skill.

Freedom you earn and freedom deserve.
You, the creature no longer serve.
In all things, I love you." (1)

Suddenly, Greg sat erect. "That is my mother," he said. "Yes, it's true. Every mother loves her baby."

During that session, he forgave his mother, and the forgiveness was complete. Indeed, he saw no need to forgive. With a new spirit of compassion, he perceived his mother as psychologically disturbed. He also saw much deeper, that in the Life Essence of her being she loved her son. She was willing to destroy her ugly, limited personality and release him to the fulfillment of his dreams. No fear, no bitterness, no hatred, no unresolved pain connected with his mother remained in him.

His inner rage and his use of abusive language gave way to constructive ways through which to express his energies. Eventually he started his own business and soon became a leading graphic artist in the area. Today, he is a Freelance Multimedia Producer.

Shortly after Greg forgave his mother, the holiday season arrived. His parents and younger brother, who still lived at home, expected him for Thanksgiving dinner. For the first time, he felt relaxed about the family eating together. After the meal, Greg's mother asked to speak with him privately. Freed from any foreboding or tension, he agreed. They secluded themselves in a room apart from the family.

"Son," she said, "for many weeks, I've been thinking about the way I treated you when you were a child. I know, now, that I aggravated you until you did something wrong so I'd have an excuse to beat you. Will you forgive me?"

He already had.

The following spring, due to a life-long heart
condition, Greg's mother was hospitalized for a yearly
check-up. Greg called me and said that his mother's
tests were over and our prayers had been answered
in the best possible way. She was well, and the doctor
planned on dismissing her Monday morning.

"Rev. Dana," Greg asked, "will you come to the
hospital to see my mother?"

Because of the family's former attitude toward
me, I hesitated. "Are you sure she wants me to? I'll
gladly come, but hasn't her own minister been
there?"

"He has come, more than once. I don't understand this either, but she asked to see you."

"Of course, I'll come. Sunday after church service, I'll be there. "

When I arrived, members of the family were talking with the nurse in the waiting room. One at a
time the relatives had been keeping her company.
The nurse left and returned saying that Greg's
mother was alone and ready to see me.

Hardly knowing what I would be led to do or say,
I entered and approached the bed where the pretty
woman in her early forties lay. We chatted about in-
consequential things. She felt fine, and the hospital
care had been good. Her doctor was wonderful, and
she looked forward to going home early the next
day. Our conversation continued with gratitude to
God for her health until I sensed that our time together was drawing to a close.

I picked up my purse and turned to move toward the door.

"Please, wait just a moment," she said.

The urgency in her quiet voice required my full
attention. Our eyes met and she took my hand.

"Rev. Dana," she continued, "I just want to thank you for doing for my boy what I couldn't do for him myself. "

We were two women, then, who knew each other on an unutterably basic level. Every mother—biological and spiritual—loves her baby although no words or actions can fully express that love. The compassion and peace we shared are comparable only to the sense of fulfillment I experienced. Spirit had moved throughout every one of Greg's symbolic, eidetic experiences during our months of work. Without a word being spoken, Spirit within Greg had connected with Spirit within his mother. All parents have the potential of being wholesome, because all are created in the image-likeness. Despite her previous outward disapproval and with no specific knowledge of the work we were doing, she had been influenced by her son's God-given visions. She had accepted full responsibility for her abuse and limitations as a mother. She had sought forgiveness and expressed her gratitude. Thus, the activity of Spirit healed her tormented soul.

While asleep, during the wee hours of the next morning, she released her physical body and returned home to her Creator.

Following is the authorization that I received from Greg to use his case study:

> Dearest Dana;
> Thank you so much for honoring me with your request. When I read your letter, I was flooded with feelings that I had buried under years of daily routines. I had forgotten our sessions, but I will never forget the

effects. I am convinced that your work with me through Eidetics saved my life, my very soul. You are most welcome to use any and all the information you collected from me during our sessions.

I grant not only permission, but accompany it with a prayer: "May the words you write and the works you accomplish bless all others as they have blessed me. "

As for my "professional title" and current work, it can be summarized briefly: I am a Freelance Producer (multimedia, to be exact), and I am proud to have been a part of helping others start various ministries—all because you took the time to dredge my soul up from the sewage I once considered my life. I am still writing short poems from the soul, and short stories (and recently started working on several short videos). These efforts would not have been possible without your therapeutic work.

Although Karen and I are all too preoccupied with our lives and the children to be in contact with you, in all honesty there is hardly a day that goes by that I don't think of you. What I find interesting is that when we do speak, it is as though we spoke only a few days prior. What you have done for me bridges the gap of time . . . perhaps that is what being a friend means, after all.

God bless you and your endeavors, Greg
(Karen, Jessica and Sara) (2)

We know, dear Reader, that nothing Good could

have happened had Spirit not been working through all of us.

For Your Spirit, Lord, we are forever grateful. Amen.

A Guided Eidetic Meditation: Releasing Wounds of the Soul

Be still, dear One. Let your personal thoughts and feelings go. Your personal thoughts and feelings may be mistaken. God is never mistaken. Release control. Your plans may be limiting. Your will and determination can be harmful. God is expansive, creative and never harmful or limiting.

Allow yourself, your entire self to move easily into the Life Essence of your being. You are resting now, quietly and calmly. Your Father-Mother-Creator is right here, waiting to help you and support you, waiting to tell you what to say and do in every situation.

Know this: Your biological parents are not your True Parents. You came through them physically for this earth-walk only.

Accept this unblemished Truth: God is your True Parent, and you are the Beloved Image-Likeness. God as universal Principle, the Law of being, is your Holy Father. God, as Divine Love, the Nurturer, is your Virgin Mother. Right now you are being offered guidance from the Truth of your being and from unconditional Love.

Relax and be at ease. Go deeper, deeper than ever before. There is nothing to fear.

Honestly and openly look into your deepest self. Do you harbor hurt feelings involving someone for whom you care, someone with whom you yearn for reconciliation? Is there someone from whom you want understanding, perhaps even love and acceptance?

See yourself, now with this person. Release your fears, your reasons for hesitating. Your Divine Mother and your Holy Father are with you, protecting you and enfolding you with wisdom and compassion. Take your time. The Light of God shines in you and throughout the entire situation. Experience the other person's presence.

In the silence of this vision, let your feelings speak for themselves. Quietly, with the support of your True Parents tell your loved one, your friend, your acquaintance, or whomever it may be, of the hurt and concern that lies heavy on your heart.

How does the other react? Is there surprise? Is there resistance? What does the other one say or do?

Watch and listen. Do not try to analyze. Your Father is your guidance as to *what* you are to say and *what* you are to do. Your Mother is the Love moving through your heart, expressing *understanding* in what you say and *compassion* in what you do.

What is happening in this sacred vision? What is going on between you and the other person? There is no need for personal control. This is the movement of Spirit within you. Allow the vision to flow as it will.

Watch as Spirit in your loved one responds and unites with Spirit in you. Does your dear one want to remain close right now? Does your friend need some space and time? Do you need some space and time? Is it time for you to move on?

Whatever it is, don't force the outcome of this experience. Just let it be. You are given these visions by God. Universal Spirit is active. You are being guided moment by moment. And so it is that you are at peace.

Thank You, Father-Mother-Creator, that this is so. Amen.

Your personal world, dear One, is a reflection of your consciousness. After slowly experiencing this meditation once a day for several days, there will be changes in your thoughts and feelings. If you are to say anything in the outer, God will open the door and speak loving words through you to the other. Your attitude will change from one of hurt and of struggle to even the score to one of acceptance and compassion. Only Good will come in your relationship with this person for whom you care. Only Good *can* come because you are One with God.

Chapter 2

AWAKENING TO THE ACTIVITY OF SPIRIT

Fashioned from the earth, we are souls in clay
form.
> *We need to remain in rhythm with our inner*
> *clay voice and longing.*
> > John O'Donohue (1)

There is a consciousness that, until recently, has
been regarded as the exclusive domain of holy
men, clergy, avatars and divine healers—the chosen
few. What a revelation to realize that it is available to
each of us, individually. We can think of this as an
inner Life Essence that is pure and that nothing can
destroy or change. Besides encompassing our individual and universal connection with the Most High,
it embraces our individual and universal clay-like,
earth connection with all that is, including all lowly

forms of life and all apparently inanimate manifestations. Thus, it offers us, not only the grander, more
expansive dimension of living, it also retains the pri-
mordial kinship we have with each other. It is a consciousness that expresses itself through something
other than the energy common to our usual space-
time experience and control.

From the seventeenth century until the development of quantum mechanics during the 1920s,
the idea of invisible forces affecting objects at a distance was discounted by scientists. According to psi
researcher, Dean Radin, author of *The Conscious Universe*, physicists regarded such phenomenon as irrational religious notions about spirits. However, they
needed an explanation for such occurrences. So they
"imagined forces as acting on objects through the
exchange of energy packets, much like colliding bil-
liard balls.(2)

Radin continues, "Quantum fields do not exist
physically in space-time like the classically inferred
gravitational and electromagnetic fields. Instead,
quantum fields specify only probabilities for strange,
ghostlike particles as they manifest in space-time.
Although quantum fields are mathematically similar
to classical fields, they are more difficult to understand because, unlike classical fields, they exist outside the usual boundaries of space-time. This gives
the quantum field a peculiar nonlocal character,
meaning the field is not located in a given region of
space and time. With a nonlocal phenomenon, what
happens in region A instantaneously influences what
occurs in region B, and vice versa, without any energy being exchanged between the two regions. Such
a phenomenon would be impossible according to
classical physics, and yet, nonlocality has been dra-

matically and convincingly revealed in modern physics experiments."(2)

For years some people have healed others, even at a distance, by entering this consciousness during what is called intercessory prayer. They have done so without having any scientific explanation for their successes and without having any scientific means of evaluating and comparing their successful and their unsuccessful attempts. Their failures have often been attributed to lack of faith in God or to God's will, rather than to the need to develop useful methods of entering a consciousness that is devoid of space-time limitations.

Somehow, scientific validation of our spiritual beliefs is strengthening. Jesus Christ said, "I and the Father are One" (John 10:30). Christ was alive in the man, Jesus. Perhaps God's intention, after all, is that we learn to know as God knows and become—through such knowledge correctly used—like God, ourselves. Christ is alive in each one of us, today. Jesus Christ is Lord of this world and has taken on the responsibility for its people.

When Jesus said, "All authority in heaven and on earth has been given to me" (Matthew 28:18), was he not speaking through his Christed Self? And was not the Spirit of the Most Ancient One, our Creator, moving through the author of Isaiah 9:6-7? That scripture reads, "For to us a child is born, to us a son is given, and the government will be on his shoulders. And he will be called Wonderful Counselor, Mighty God, Everlasting Father, Prince of Peace. Of the increase of his government and peace there will be no end." Let us, in all our comings and goings, remember that Christ is within everyone who walks this earth, no matter the race, faith or philosophy. It is His sacred Truth in every individual that each of us eventually will discover and willingly, passionately follow.

The evidence of science and religion reaching agreements is piecemeal and tentative, but it is there. Science confirms what Shiva, the Hindu god of construction and destruction, has symbolized for centuries; nothing is gained except at the price of an equivalent loss. This reinforces the Christian belief that we each must release our life as we have known it in order to receive a higher consciousness and greater fulfillment. For instance, today more than ever before, we are becoming involved in the well being of others on a personal, national and global scale. To do so, many are turning away from our society's obsession with self-absorption. I see my students moving beyond their inhibitions, accepting the scars of their healed wounds and taking on more magnanimous attitudes and life-styles. This is the activity of Spirit moving in and through individual souls.

It's your choice. You, too, can involve yourself in Spirit's divine intention to move through you while you serve in your world. Your choice may arise in the midst of a difficult situation or relationship in which the spoken word has no constructive influence.

The contrast between healing with and without an openness to the activity of Spirit is dramatic. At a time when contemporary psychology has been promoting confrontation as a means of changing the balance of power between parents and grown children, my counselees have welcomed a more expansive solution. During overt confrontation, separation usually becomes greater, the wall becomes higher and the one confronting, though more in control, develops only a smidgen of compassion—if any.

However, through God-given visions, Spirit in anyone can speak silently to Spirit in another, healing psychological wounds in both. Indeed, as shown in the case study in Chapter 1, broken relationships can be restored without a word of blame or accusation being spoken. Honoring one's parents, as the Old Testament Bible commands, is to recognize that they, too, are worthy of being healed.

You are created to become a wholesome Human Being—two words that should, I think, be capitalized because all humans are sacred. Were it not for Spirit moving within and expressing as you, you would not be here at all. In a sweeping view of the world, spiritual growth seems almost nonexistent. And probably you will agree that for the individual, soul growth usually seems too gradual. We appear to be less than our divine potential. Our responsibility is to recognize our "less than" areas, to uproot them at their source and to heal any psychological pain and resulting physical ailments they have caused.

In your Life Essence you are Perfection, you are the Most Ancient Consciousness. There, you can silently relive and restore any psychic injury you have experienced. You have an innate ability to heal past trauma and recreate your memory with the divine Truth, the Image in which God created you. Sacred visions are just as available, today, as to ancient men and women of all faiths. The mission of each vision is to heal, to free your captive energies and thus to renew, enrich and direct the fulfilling of your life.

We need to know that emotions such as anger, frustration, sadness, helplessness and grief are God-given. Why are they not treated as such? For one reason, the culture in which we live has long repressed negative feelings and, therefore, has fostered

denial of depression, anger, fear, etc. We have become clever at hiding our emotions under poor self-
esteem. Who can think well of herself when she is
ashamed of valid feelings?

From the beginning we have been blessed with
feelings. Without fear and anger, the caveman could
not have protected his family against wild animals
and enemy tribes. Can you imagine a cave man pas-
sively sitting by while a lion devoured his family? Without adrenaline racing through his body, that's what
he would have done.

Today, when you experience fear and anger,
chances are that you are not in the danger of being
killed that our early ancestors were. Today, even
physical abuse can be stopped with the help of proper
authorities. Seventy years ago that was not the norm.
Incest and beatings were secret family business,
hushed behind closed mouths and locked doors.

However, there is psychological danger, today,
from others' immaturity and from corruption in high
places. To protect yourself, as we have said, requires
the transmutation of negative emotions. Only then
can you utilize the underlying energies to make
changes and to live constructively with your relationships and in your world.

To reiterate, it is in the stillness of one's Life Essence that souls can be healed. There, you can harm-
lessly express the negative emotions that you experienced as a child toward adult role models or that
you experience, today, toward whomever. Your Father-Mother-Creator comprehends your reason and
knows your need. In symbolic activity, rather than in
overt confrontation that could alienate the other and
worsen the situation, Spirit is present and active.
There are no limitations then. Spirit within you car-

ries what cannot be said in words to Spirit in the other. Thus, motivation for that one's enlightenment and for reconciliation between the two of you is established. This process is carried forward in succeeding chapters. It is just as science is proving: When an individual gives undivided attention to anything, animate or inanimate, the object of that attention changes.

We can liken human growth to the classic example of the acorn developing into an oak tree. Every living thing has the image within of its potential wholeness. However, if an acorn does not receive enough nourishment from the earth, warmth from the sun and rain from the sky, it develops into a twisted, stunted tree. Just so, when a child does not receive proper parental nourishment and guidance, it grows into a dysfunctional adult.

In this process, we do not decide intellectually how we want a vision to develop. Instead we enter the Life Essence of our being where we accept and follow the first image that accompanies any eidetic situation. We do not analyze; God guides us in symbolism that is clear, easy to follow and often humorous. We love symbolism because we recognize that Divinity finds expression in this fascinating form. Thus, like the acorn naturally developing into a sturdy oak, we become our divine potential. Simultaneously, the etheric thread of Spirit connects with and influences others involved to do the same.

When awakening to the activity of Spirit, start by cleansing your own thoughts and feelings. You can hold not only yourself, but also others back with your negative attitudes about them. If they are not strong enough in consciousness to know that no one, outside of themselves, can keep their good from them, they will get caught in your negative energy so that the two of you swim around in it together, like two fish in a bowl of unclean water.

Similarly, to allow negative thoughts and fears for a loved one to take hold of your consciousness multiplies and intensifies the fear, itself. On the other hand, an immediate connection with God, knowing that God is in the situation and that only good can come, reaches forth with divine order into your loved one's life.

One Saturday afternoon at 12:55, a woman had a frightening sense that her daughter, who had traveled to a remote, inaccessible region across the country, was in grave danger. The remainder of Saturday and all the next day, Sunday, she prayed the following "Prayer of Protection" by Unity poet, James Dillet Freeman:

> The Light of God surrounds you;
> The Love of God enfolds you;
> The Power of God protects you;
> The Presence of God watches over you.
> Wherever you are, God is! (3)

Not knowing where the daughter was staying, she waited, keeping what early New Thought teachers referred to as the High Watch. Sunday evening her daughter called. "Mother," she said "I've got to tell you what happened. Yesterday our car was almost hit by a train. All of us could have been killed!" When asked what time it happened, she said that it was just before one p.m.

We hear and read in today's news of similar circumstances, too many to brush off as coincidence or an overactive imagination. Because of scientific research, we now understand that miracles are the wondrous activity of Spirit in heretofore unrecognized natural laws.

One of my student's experiences clearly demonstrates that the combination of space and time is no deterrent to Spirit. Sydney, a successful artist, was estranged from her wealthy mother, a widow, who lived in another state. Her first memories were of being ignored, although the mother lavished attention and generosity on a son, the younger child. This continued during their adulthood with the mother giving large sums of money to the son and nothing, financial or otherwise, to the daughter.

For years, the artist struggled with bitterness and, finally, was able to forgive. She yearned for acceptance and appreciation from her mother, often prayerfully surrounding her mother with the Light of God and envisioning the two of them, together, looking at Sydney's prize paintings. Every attempt for outer communication, however, was met with coldness. When the artist received an invitation to show her work in Paris, her husband gave her money to ship the paintings, but she had no airfare for herself.

One week before she had to confirm her appearance in Paris, her mother called. She said she felt an urgent need to send several hundred dollars to her daughter. Would she accept it? The mother had always been interested in art and when she found out what the money would be used for, she was delighted. She not only sent travel expenses for the Paris trip, she later sent a gift of $10,000 each to Sydney and to her brother.

As Sydney demonstrated, we possess a fine spiritual bond with one another. When we forgive an injustice and prayerfully envision a loving, wholesome connection with the other, the relationship changes. Any vision can be your unspoken decree and it shall be established for you.

We are blessed in so many ways that no previous generation has been. We are in an era, now, when we can and shall be aware of much deeper spiritual connections with one another than we ever have experienced before.

Pay attention. You will meet someone for the first time, perhaps look into that person's eyes and discover a surprising, inexplicable depth of recognition there. This is not to question, analyze or attempt to rationalize. If you should think, "Well, we have been together in another lifetime, probably," you will have diminished its mysterious, intrinsic value. Let it be and you will develop a reverence for the solid foundation of your mutual clay beginnings, for the radiant living substance from which we all come.

Someone who became momentarily acquainted with me on this soul level has affected not only my entire life but, also, those to whom I have ministered. She was one of several experienced ministers sitting with me around a long conference table, interviewing me to receive my ordination. The great aura of power and success seemed especially centered around two men in the group. I learned later that they sometimes employed unique tactics when talking with unsuspecting prospective ministers. Before I entered the room, they had decided to collaborate in an attempt to stump me with perplexing theological questions. In struggling to keep pace with their confounding queries and remarks, I began to feel intimidated. Sitting next to me, a woman minis-

ter quietly placed her hand on my arm. With that
moment's caring touch I regained my composure.

After the meeting this minister, whom I regard
as one of my greatest teachers, met me in the hall-
way. We talked briefly. But her words have remained
with me throughout my life, especially when I have
been serving and counseling others. "Look into the
other's soul," she said, "rather than at the personality and the physical appearance."

Through following her guidance, I have come to
understand what I am attempting to explain to you
now. Only by seeing and knowing another's soul and
by loving the movement of Spirit therein, can you
truly relate and minister to the profound, internal
needs of another. The courageous coming together
of two souls is a sacred activity. Spirit once separated
you and since has been drawing you together again
in a finer union. In the Most Ancient Mind, we have
existed from the beginning and will continue
through all eternity.

I write to all people, no matter the age. I write to
anyone seeking or experiencing love. We yearn for
close relationships, but nothing lasting can be forced.
In every friendship, a caring, watchful objectivity
unfolds the intimacy intended by the Father-Mother-
Creator.

When you are with someone whose soul you recognize and you must part, regardless of the reason,
know that the pure love you feel is a bond between
you that will never break. Love is eternal. To love
without visible evidence of its return does not diminish its value in your heart and psyche. Love because
it is your nature to love, not because you decide by
whom and when your love is to be returned.

Students come to me afraid that a relationship

will not last. There is nothing to fear. Only receive your guidance from your highest consciousness, so that love's goodness and purity can enrich your eternal life on earth and in Heaven. Give your soul room to breathe.

The Gospel According To Thomas, expresses Heaven's qualifications best:

20 (22) Jesus saw children who were being suckled. He said to his disciples: These children who are being suckled

22 are like those who enter the Kingdom. They said to Him: Shall we then, being children,

24 enter into the Kingdom? Jesus said to them: When you make the two one, and

26 when you make the inner as the outer and the outer as the inner and the above

28 as the below, and when you make the male and the female into a single one,

30 so that the male will not be male and the female (not) be female, when you make

32 eyes in the place of an eye, and a hand in the place of a hand, and a foot in the place

34 of a foot, (and) an image in the place of an image, then shall you enter [the Kingdom].

Log. 22; Pages 17, 19(4)

Our attraction to the opposite sex is so natural that to say sexual activity is commendable and desirable would be redundant. What is commendable and necessary, though, is that we use our sexual energies wisely and appropriately. Sexual fulfillment, in its finest expression, is attuned to Spirit. However, during soul to soul communication, our single-minded eyes perceive only Good in all, our hands and feet serve God's grand, cosmic plan and our images arise from a pure heart. Gender is of no importance. The male will not be male and the female will not be female. When sacred Love comes your way, with or without sexual intimacy, neither space nor time nor physical death can diminish or destroy it.

Soul interaction moves in another dimension that, rather than discounting the physical, assumes the holiness of the body temple. With such a relationship, we perceive our mutual beginnings and somehow relate more easily with the wisdom, love and compassion that Jesus exemplified. This is not always easy to do, nor can we force or determine the relationship's outcome. Its great rewards arrive unexpectedly in the joy of accepting what is. The mysterious unfolding and molding of separated clay-united soul entities is beyond our comprehension or control. Let it, dear Friend, ring in your heart without your rigid determination. Become as a little child.

When I was about ten years old, a favorite aunt gave me a book titled, *Grey Sprite and the Silver Knight.* At the time, I was carried away into another realm by the relationship between two earth-bound characters in the story: an oak tree and a vine, living side by side in a great forest. I read the book over and over and can still feel the texture of its gray-blue cover. In this fable the oak developed strength and honor, and the gentle vine grew in purity and wisdom. Symbolically they demonstrated for my young mind the innate need and desire we have to care for one another.

While working with my students, the following

Eidetic formed from the memory of this childhood experience with the oak tree and the vine.

A Guided Eidetic Meditation: Beginnings and Caring

When you take part in this guided eidetic meditation, savor each segment of its development. Afterwards, without following the text, experience a similar vision that is your own Eidetic. Let it be your gift from God.

Settle yourself in your favorite position. Take your time. Relax and enter the Life Essence of your being. Breathe slowly and fully. Go deeper with each breath. There is no need to strain or force anything. Your breath is the Spirit of God giving you life.

When you are ready, my Friend, experience yourself as an acorn. You are cradled deep in the womb of your Mother the Earth. Blanketed in the comfort of darkness, you are given all the nourishment and moisture you could possible want. And you are given this, without your asking.

Ever so gradually you respond to an urge to reach out. Your fragile tentacles spread forth grasping your Mother with their tiny hold. The sustenance and strength you receive assures you that all is well. You develop firm, thick roots, strengthened by the Mother-Love that you so effortlessly receive. Earth worms crawl around you, twining and circling along.

Soon something lures you, entices you upward. An unaccustomed warmth and light permeates the cool darkness. You sprout through your Mother-Earth's surface and are stimulated, delighted by the rays of the sun. Your Father the Sky guides you and directs you, sending sunbeams to warm you, sending rain to quench your thirst and gentle breezes to cool you. Thunder, lightning, and mighty winds bend you and make you strong.

Your home is a forest, a grand stand of oaks and kindred trees. Shrubs and grasses, wild flowers and ferns carpet the ground. Little critters and animals scamper here and there. You are branching out now, stalwart, fearless, courageous. You sprout an abundance of leaves and give birth to baby acorns. Birds seek shelter and nest among your branches.

As you continue to mature, something strange occurs. A gentle sensation moving along your trunk does not feel like bugs or caterpillars or anything that you know.

Creeping upward, sensing and clinging to the crevices of your trunk, a little vine entwines herself upward and around. A comfortable sense of belonging, of being of great value warms your heart.

Her leaves whisper, "Thank you for your support."
And you respond, "I'm so glad to be of service."

Thank You, Father-Mother-Creator, for our clay beginnings. Amen.

An Eidetic Meditation

Now, Friend, when you are ready, experience a similar vision that is your own.

Let it be an eidetic vision. This means that you do not decide in advance what is to take place. That would be a vision for your intellect. An Eidetic rejuvenates the soul.

Simply become the first seed, or kernel or whatever it is in nature that moves you. Experience yourself slowly growing into maturity. Savor each segment of your development.

Enrich your life by inviting a caring relationship with another wild, untouched, living bit of nature. This vision is your sacred gift from God. Thank You, God. Thank You. Amen.

John O'Donohue, the Celtic poet and author of *Anam Cara*, celebrates our clay beginnings:

"Often the joy you feel does not belong to your individual biography but to the clay out of which you are formed." (5)

"To truly be and become yourself, you need the ancient radiance of others."(5)

Chapter 3

THE CHOICE IS YOURS—OR IS IT?

*I have set before you life and death, blessings
and curses.
Now choose life, so that you and your children may live.*

Deuteronomy 30:19

The thirty-five-year-old man sat curled in a fetal
position on my office couch, sobbing. Alienation
from his parents because of sexual abuse when he
was a child, a series of unfortunate intimate relationships, demanding work in a government position and
the stress of study to further his education had shat-
tered his spirit. He was good looking, exceptionally
intelligent and suicidal. An added tragedy was that
his fundamental religious background offered guilt
rather than solace and healing. Due to some serious

mistakes which he had made and regarded as unforgivable sins, he expected, even welcomed his depression. "I deserve to be punished," he told me.

Over the centuries, Adam and Eve have been condemned as the humans who first committed "original sin." Now, this young man was experiencing, in full bloom, what he perceived to be the results of his own original sin. Not only had it separated him from his biological parents but echoing the ancient allegory, from his spiritual Father-Mother-God as well. Yet, by his presence in my office, he was choosing to live.

We could research and analyze pages of intellectual discussion about Adam and Eve, the snake and the two trees in the Garden of Eden. Thank Goodness I have the freedom of choice, and I choose not to. If you believe in evolution you can appreciate the symbolic Truth in a classic tale that has been around for so many years that I'm sure, some of you have heard it.

A Sunday School teacher asked the children to draw pictures of their favorite Bible stories. Johnny brought a picture to her of an old man, with a flowing white beard, seated behind the wheel of a red sport car. In the back seat two teenagers, a boy and a girl, sat laughing and carrying on. When the teacher asked Johnny to explain his picture, he said, "See, this man in the driver's seat? That's God, and he's driving Adam and Eve out of the Garden of Eden."

There is symbolic Truth in this story. Just now, I have another story to tell. One that actually happened. It illustrates our power to manifest the antithesis of Truth if we so choose.

Years ago while in my first ministry, the teenagers in my congregation told me of houses in the city where black magic and witchcraft were being practiced. Some had experimented with these forces and obviously were both fascinated and apprehensive. A dark energy pervaded the city.

One night my office phone rang. It was very late. A terrified, middle-aged woman answered, begging me to pray for her. She had become curious about the "lower entities" as she called them, that the kids had been talking about. For several nights, before sleeping, she had asked these entities to visit her so she would know whether or not they were real. During the previous two nights, dark, menacing, evil creatures *had* appeared, standing momentarily at the foot of her bed. She had tried to calm herself by passing the experiences off as the activity of her vivid imagination. But the third night, just before she called me, her husband had seen them too! The terror in her voice cannot be described. I prayed aloud with her, using the same "Prayer of Protection" that is mentioned in Chapter 2:

> The light of God surrounds you;
> The love of God enfolds you;
> The power of God protects you;
> The presence of God watches over you.
> Wherever you are, God is! (1)

Early the next morning, she came to my office after a night of drifting in and out of restless sleep. We prayed together again. We talked about the power of the mind and the necessity of focusing on God rather than on "Satan" or his cohorts. We can, *of course*, manifest Satan if we so choose. After that night, she and her husband continued to use the "Prayer of Protection" especially before going to bed. The dark entities did not return.

We now have two different stories that seem to be related. Let's take another look at the presence of good and evil in our lives today as well as in the lives of those in the Garden of Eden.

While the little boy's story mentioned above is cute, it is symbolically meaningful, just as meaningful as the illustration of the woman and the evil entities is. Our Creator, naturally present and active within each one, *is driving* us with urges and curiosities too insistent and promising to be ignored. Our human mental and physical activity always has been and is now the vehicle for the inherent maturing process through which God's grace redeems us. Today, we examine the value of this activity and see that we are blessed with the ability to discriminate and with the freedom of choice between two possibilities. We can seek knowledge of good and evil as the woman in the above illustration did and as Adam and Eve did or we can focus on God and everlasting life.

Lacking a well-developed faculty of discrimination and bursting with curiosity, the mythical first male and female responded to the next step in their evolutionary growth. They moved forward with what understanding they had at the time. This understanding was controversial, caused by their introduction to evil and their experience of God (Good). Their freedom of choice came with a price—the responsibility of depending on their own efforts and wit for survival.

As we move into the new millennium, we are beginning to grasp that the extent and value of *our* freedom corresponds with our willingness to work with the potential good inherent in all of life's gifts. When we consciously choose to grow spiritually, we are nourished by the tree of Life, and we strive to see no evil in any of creation, even in the other tree.

Blessing or Cursing: Which Will It Be?

So it is, my Friend, that along with your freedom to choose, you are constantly presented with opportunities to bless or to curse. It is as you give that you receive. Do you perceive the good, the pure and the beautiful—in other words, are you aware of God, the Good, in all that exists? When Adam and Eve started to investigate, they left behind passive blind obedience to God. What they lacked in wisdom they made up in teenage-like nerve and courage to step out on their own. How about you, with today's understanding of this dilemma? Have you released your passive, blind obedience to the indoctrination others have imposed upon you about God? Have you the courage to seek the Kingdom for yourself, to seek God's step by step guidance, to venture forth, make mistakes, and pick yourself up to try again?

Symbolically, the Garden story poses many questions. Are you controlled by the habit of placing blame, by lack of forgiveness and lack of compassion? Do you always have to come out on top, even at the expense of others? Are you ashamed of your body? Do you mistreat your body and the body of others? Is your body and are your senses in control of you, or do you control your bodily functions and physical senses?

In Genesis 1:31, the Creator saw "all that he had

made, and it was very good." What do you see, dear One? Your freedom lies in your perception.

When the disciples questioned Jesus as to whom could be saved, He responded, "With man this is impossible, but with God all things are possible" (Matthew 19:26). Over the years, Christianity has encumbered the word "saved" with the rigid belief that only through Jesus can anyone be "saved from original sin" and, after physical death, go to heaven and eternal life rather than to hell and eternal suffering. Christians have prayed for the seemingly impossible, for so-called "miracles" to be conferred through the whim of a far away, condemnatory and vengeful God. Some still pray in this way and, along with ignorance about God's Love, try by and for themselves to "love Jesus enough to be saved." Sometimes the pleas have been granted and sometimes not, causing the individuals to worry and wonder and doubt themselves and their Creator.

Since God is loving and forgiving, isn't the mistake we want to avoid that of hiding from Her? Are we not going astray when we stop communicating with Him? There is that in us all that yearns for divine Love and Law and knows, in our individual souls, when we have lost sight of it.

Most people, perhaps without being aware, cling to destructive habits and attitudes. I know this to be true, because I am one who has done so in the past and, possibly, am one who still does so, today. How about you? Does dredging up your harmful thoughts and emotions and then teaching the underlying energies to flow in more constructive channels seem to be as difficult as changing the course of the Mississippi River would be? Yes or no, Friend, it is your lifelong responsibility. To fulfill that responsibility or not, the choice is yours.

Developing Compassion

When things do not unfold as we want, the human tendency is to place blame and try to even the score. However, we don't have to continue to act with the same old impulsive attitudes and actions.

Reporter David Wallechinsky relates compelling stories of compassion in an article that appeared in *The Stuart News*. He tells of three teenage girls who went to a 78-year-old grandmother's home supposedly for Bible study. Instead they stabbed the woman to death in order to get money to play arcade games. Their fifteen-year-old leader was sentenced to die.

The woman's grandson, an overhead crane operator in a steel mill, said, "If they didn't give the death penalty in my grandmother's case, than they were saying my grandmother wasn't an important person. I felt my grandmother was a very important person."

However, when he was left alone at work one day, he started thinking how his grandmother would have felt about the guilty teenager who had been severely abused as a child.

"Her parents didn't even come to the sentencing," he said. "That was the day it was decided whether she would live or die, and they didn't come." The next day he wrote to the fifteen-year-old and offered to speak out to save her from execution. She replied that it wasn't necessary. All she wanted was forgiveness.(2)

Justice without compassion lacks wisdom and is

only human justice. When seeking justice in day to day circumstances, do you vacillate between blaming yourself and blaming others? Or do you simply give up and accept any adversity as being God's will? Isn't that blaming? Making God responsible for the immature, harmful decisions you make is a cop-out. Rather than blaming God, eagerly accept your own responsibilities, use your God-given talents to manifest health, financial security, happiness, peace of mind and loving relationships. When you put your mind and heart into following your deep, inner guidance, every good thing will be yours.

Furthermore, committing yourself to acting through your Christed Self gives you wisdom to learn from mistakes and, thus, become more open to Spirit. For instance, if you use God's gifts in destructive ways, discord always results, so you decide you can do better. God gives you life, substance and intelligence. What you do with these sacred gifts is your choice.

Ask yourself, "Why is it necessary to place blame at all?" A bad choice, made by anyone, is just a bad choice. Behind the most appalling actions, there is an ignorance, an injury of some sort, hiding the love of God that is waiting to heal the perpetrator. Compassion develops with understanding.

A counselor friend of mine declared that he would counsel anyone excepting a child abuser. He harbored only contempt for such a person but soon found that whatever he resisted became a strong part of his experience. His superior referred a male child molester to him for counseling. In getting to know the individual, who had been abused himself during his formative years, my friend realized that the man was aware of no other way of loving. The compassion this counselor eventually felt for him led to transfor-

mational sessions, not only for the man who came
for healing but also for the healer himself.

To Seek the Kingdom

To confuse justice with rejection, with refusal to
forgive and/or with motivation to even the score accomplishes only on the karmic plane. Can't we find
a better way? Why can't we simply accept life as it
unfolds, regardless of present circumstances? Why
can't we trust the universe to somehow open the way
for our Good to come to us, no matter what someone else thinks or does? Not that we never will feel
gut reactions such as fear and anger. But we will conserve the energy of such emotions until all the facts,
our meditative work, our enlightened thought and
the appropriate timing come together, and we can
express with wisdom. All this preparatory work is
seeking the Kingdom of God, which is not found in
our intuition alone, our feelings alone or in our intellect alone. It is found, sacred and shining, in the
harmony between our Christ-centered mind and
heart.

In Max Freedom Long's *The Secret Science at Work,*
the author writes of the ancient Huna teaching: "To
'seek the kingdom' means 1. to learn that there is a
High Self, 2. to come to a rational belief in its existence and in the fact that it is willing and able to help
us, and 3. to learn by practice to cause the low self to
contact the High Self by means of the aka cord, and
to present the mana and the prayer.

"In the simple words of Huna, one may say, 'First
learn to contact the High Self in its level above you,
and if you can do this successfully, your prayers can

be delivered and all things which you can gain through the use of prayer will be given you.'" (3)

In Western research and practice, much applause has been given to psychiatry and to New Thought philosophy for their teachings of three levels of consciousness: the lower, subconscious; the middle, conscious; and the higher, Divine or Christ Consciousness. A study of these teachings helps us recall that the original element of our physical body was dust, clay all lumped together. Our Father-Mother-Creator conceived us, has moved through us from our genesis and, today, is still working His/Her evolutionary mystery through human beings and all of creation. It is as though we are ascending an evolutionary staircase. The bottom step represents our clay beginnings and the top symbolizes the *Kingdom*. Partway up the stairs isn't at the bottom and it isn't at the top, but it is the stair where we always stop, pausing for our present momentous manifestation.

However, when we regard ourselves as *only* human with three parts, we forgo the shining mysterious single-eyed wonder that views our sacred growth as primarily the activity of Spirit. Even our choice to move at all originates at the urging of Spirit. On the other hand, when we try to dishonor our humanness and put forth great effort and energy to make ourselves only Divine, we miss the immeasurable joy of the human experience. To sum up: by putting forth unflinching conscious analysis and effort to reach the top of the stairs, we forget that Spirit is and always has been evolving us, and not we ourselves. All we can do is remain open to the Sacred. Through Spirit—active in our entire being—much happens in our psyche of which we are not cognizant, but Spirit alters our perception, nonetheless.

The eidetic experience is spiritual and takes place in our Life Essence, which impregnates every aspect of our being. Within it, space/time simply does not exist and intellectual discussion and determination—if their intrusion were possible—would be ineffective. Eidetics works in the Life Essence, simultaneously, with all three so-called levels of consciousness.

In the words of Dr. Akhter Ahsen, "The instrument of volitional thinking is words, but the instrument of the life process is the eidetic, which appears in consciousness to educate and transform the individual. The biolatency (the encoded descriptions of positive life impressions in the organism gifted through genetic endowment) of the eidetic process changes the very thought processes of the individual. The ego in its best ordinary states is able to have only fleeting moments of life intermixed with inevitable feelings of limitation. However, when the ego opens itself to the nonconscious biolatency process to what lies beyond its limiting horizon, it experiences a luminous opening. Parts of the mind outside of the ego enter the ego and break its limitations and containment, initiating a nourishing orientation to life." (4)

For instance, when a soul has been mutilated, the wounded portion is shut down and hidden from one's awareness. We can liken eidetic activity to Kirlian photography in which the image of the broken off part of a leaf is captured on a negative, developed and brought into view. And so it is with a soul injury. Through one's eidetic experience of concentration and repetition the luminous activity of Spirit reveals, cherishes and heals the mutilated part of the human psyche. With this inner activity, the original, uncontaminated healing energy of God is set free.

As mentioned before, so much strain is caused simply by folks who do not know who they are and measure themselves only as human or struggle to become only Divine. The wonder is that we are both and that Creation forever intends us to be right where we are in Spirit. Humility before the Most Ancient One requires that we accept the activity of Spirit in our clay-like beginnings as well as now. We do not know what constant Oneness will be, nor will we know until we are there. Furthermore, in such sacred surroundings any attempt to verbalize our Oneness would be more than redundant or an infraction, it would be impossible. However, when we know who we are, Spirit is there to move more freely through us, simply because we are open.

A woman called me one evening wanting an appointment. I had an opening the next day, but she cried with such distress that I agreed to see her during my dinner hour. She told me she had multiple personalities—nine of them—and did not call her psychiatrist whom she liked, because she wanted spiritual counseling. She had no religious affiliation.

During the two-hour session, we talked about God and prayed. Of course, we all play different roles in life. She agreed that she was a daughter, a sister, an ex-wife, a divorced single mom, etc. We talked about these roles being outer expressions and, in a way, similar to the nine personalities that she acted out. I explained that although the nine personalities seemed very real in her mind and actions, she had only one true identity, and that was as God imaged and created her. No matter what she did or what role she acted out and no matter what ever happened to her, God's image of her was the only true Self. Furthermore, that true Self would always dwell in the Life Essence of her being, just as the image of the oak tree lives in the acorn. She said no one had ever told her that before and left, adding, "You have saved my life. I was planning on committing suicide tonight." She called two days later, still feeling much better.

I've seen her since and one time she told me that she just came from her psychiatrist's and that he thinks she is doing well. We know that it was the movement of Spirit within and between both of us, not Dana J. Voght, who saved her life that one evening.

Spiritual Isolation Is Not the Way to Go

Too often, our culture's healing practices discount or ignore the spiritual isolation that causes illnesses. Oh, that everyone would realize that the Kingdom of God is within. For many Christians, there seems to be a gap between life and the Principles taught by Jesus. I'm sure that there are those in other faiths who find the same void between their everyday experiences and Principles they have been taught. It is within this perceived gap that most people try to control their own and others' lives, rather than seeking inner spiritual guidance.

One man believed that doing God's will was deciding *rationally* what it was and then willing himself to do it. Having had a fundamentalist upbringing, he believed the more he suffered, the more acceptable he was to God. Once he told me, "I want to

suffer as much as Jesus suffered," which he is trying
to do mentally, emotionally and physically.

Do you sometimes try intellectually to decide for
yourself what is good for you and for those around
you and then ruthlessly pursue your rationalization?
The good perceived by some to be the will of God
falls far short of that which is good for everyone.

During her teens, one of my students already had
a promising singing voice. Her father, an unsuccessful opera star, paid for her singing lessons and, as
she grew older, scheduled her performances and
managed her singing career. When she met and fell
in love with a young man, he soon proposed. The
father objected to the marriage, and my student
stopped seeing her friend socially, although she could
not avoid him professionally. Her father continued
to push her, "to encourage her," he said. But finally,
she had a breakdown. For months, they did not
speak. Eventually, she told her father she never
wanted to sing in public again. He did not accept his
part in her breakdown and subsequent decision. She,
on the other hand, decided to follow her spiritual
guidance: She married her longtime suitor.

Releasing personal control entails doing away with
the foundation upon which you stand and base your
decisions, the foundation you have built with your
human mind alone. Changing is not easy. It's more
comfortable to remain in control by altering situations, pressuring other people, even undermining
others in order to achieve what you want. When you
have to *convince* yourself that something you want to
do is God's will and not our own, without a doubt,
you are glorifying your human ego.

Years ago, when I counseled prison inmates in
Lansing, Michigan, a thirty-some year old lifer told

me that, yes, he had murdered a man. Then he explained the many "good" reasons for having done
so. He had to do it, he said, because he was desperate and had no choice. We always have a choice, even
when a circumstance appears to be hopeless. Desperation and despair generate feelings of inadequacy
and fear and always point to separation from Spirit.

When circumstances or individuals challenge your
plans and actions, do you push ahead anyway? Is having your way necessary for your happiness? The Truth
is that to live fully and to express yourself freely, you
need to be open and in tune with others on a soul
level. But until you free all others to their own guidance, you will not be free yourself. When you live to
serve and empower, rather than to control your family, friends and acquaintances, Spirit communicates
with Spirit and love results.

Of course, there are those passive individuals who
seem to accept anything that comes along. Poverty,
ill health, unfulfilling relationships and aborted
dreams are all regarded by them to be God's will.
When I questioned one student as to why such experiences continue to cloud his life, he responded,
"I don't deserve any better. You can't have it all, you
know." Such an attitude usually results from unresolved feelings of guilt that, in turn, manifest as false
humility.

If you sometimes feel guilty and undeserving,
have no fear, my Friend. Remember that God does
not punish. God loves. Your awareness of this Truth
and your application of Principle determine your life
circumstances. Furthermore, when you finally realize that no one can victimize you unless you allow it,
you will perceive a Universe that always gives you

another chance: a new, more fulfilling direction. To live or not to live, the choice is yours.

Spirit's Whys and Wherefores

Where are you in consciousness? Why are you there?

First of all, are you still surrounded by negative circumstances? Do life's blessings seem to avoid you? If so, why? One reason may be that you have not discovered the wound in your soul and looked to God for guidance in healing.

One angry young man has a captivating grin and an engaging personality. Consequently, he has been married three times and divorced twice. He says he hates both his parents and rarely contacts them. Twice, his wife and four children have taken extended trips to visit relatives. When they returned the last time, he promised to go with his wife for marriage counseling. However, when the counselor referred him to a psychiatrist who could give him more intense sessions and prescribe medication for him, he refused to go anywhere at all for help. The solution, he says, is for his wife to go into a mental hospital. Everything is her fault, just as everything was his parents' fault. Needless to say, his third marriage is splitting up, simply because this very personable young man cannot admit to his need for healing.

There is a second reason we can draw traumatic, even desperate circumstances into our lives. Sometimes, unbeknownst to us, our time has come. We are ready for an epiphany, to accept a more expansive spiritual understanding than we have ever had before.

The news reporter for the Associated Press, Terry Anderson, had considered himself an atheist until shortly before he was taken prisoner, tortured and held captive in a Lebanon prison for almost seven years. While visiting England six months before his capture, a church with a tall gray spire kept catching his eye. "After a few days," he wrote in an article that appeared in Guideposts magazine, " I finally decided to walk over to the church. When I got there I pulled open the heavy oaken door, stepped in and settled in a worn pew. Looking up at the altar and cross gleaming in the shadows, I suddenly had a strong sense of coming home. This was where I belonged. I believed in God, the Father, His Son, Christ Jesus, and His Holy Spirit." (5)

In prison, he requested and was tossed a Bible, which he read from cover to cover many times. After his release on December 4, 1991, reporters asked if he could ever forgive his captors. During a moment's hesitation, he remembered the Lord's Prayer: "Our Father . . . forgive us our debts, as we also have forgiven our debtors." He answered, "Yes, as a Christian I am required to forgive, no matter how hard it may be."

"I learned so much," he continued in his article, "in those 2,455 days. For I believe pain can help us grow. Before my capture I was a brusque, arrogant, restless man. Now I like to think I have changed. I don't know what lies ahead; but whenever I need to know where my help will come from, I will recall an old church in an English town, and a worn red Bible." (5)

A third reason speaks to your attitude toward

challenge. It involves knowing that you are fully capable of serving a certain cause and of committing to it come what may. During the last century, Martin Luther King, Jr. and Mahatma Gandhi have been models of such service.

Jesus did not ask, "What did I do wrong?" His experience came to him because He did what was "right," and he knew it. He turned to his Father for all things and, thus, transcended others' irrational opinions and actions. He was prepared in consciousness for the crucifixion on the way to the resurrection. He was prepared, and God chose him to serve because He was prepared for that particular exemplary service. Jesus and the Father were and are One in consciousness.

So it is with all of us. However, these weighty examples are not given to discourage or to frighten you. One's spiritual growth often comes through quiet, loving, seemingly uneventful service in everyday situations. Please understand, dearly Beloved, that the more spiritually mature you become, the more God's grace enlightens and transforms your soul. Whatever the situation might be, He gives you the courage and the wisdom with which to follow His infallible guidance.

Your choices in life irrevocably lead you until, as Jesus Christ said, "You did not choose me, but I chose you . . ." (John 15:16). Truth gently leads you on to make your own choices, and then in the fullness of your enlightenment, Truth definitely chooses you.

You are created by a compassionate God. Your challenges are not forced on you. Experiences come to you according to your perception, according to your need to learn from the experience and according to your spiritual readiness and capability to handle a certain choice successfully.

Be aware when you do choose, though, of what choices are yours and what are not. For instance, having an automobile accident would not be your considered choice, but the accident probably is hinting to you about the influence of your nonconscious self. How you handle yourself as the result of an accident can be your conscious choice. Will you react out of control because your unresolved, destructive emotions are in control? The decision is truly yours only when you respond constructively, even lovingly, and with wisdom enough to benefit everyone.

A Guided Eidetic Meditation: Choosing Life

As you prepare for this meditation, dear One, keep this thought in mind: A decision is yours only when you choose constructively, lovingly and for the good of all.

Now be seated or lie down if you prefer. Find your comfortable position. Stretch and settle yourself as need be. Relax in the knowledge that God is with you in every situation of your life. Probably this omnipresent God is not the God you learned about from your parents or even from the church you attended when you were a child.

This is *your* God whom you experience, who writes His Word on your heart and with whom you can share everything. This is your God, your God of Goodness and Love. You know this and are thankful for His Presence. But are there times when God seems far away, even nonexistent?

For the purpose of this meditation, experience

yourself during such a time. You have intentionally decided to do this in the Life Essence of your being. There you can rise above separation from your Father-Mother-Creator. Then in later manifestation, you will easily follow your spiritual guidance.

You are now, dear One, in the basement of your soul. Memories of failures and disappointments brought you to this place. You do not *want* to wallow in despair. You seem to have no control over the bitterness that fills your mind.

One after another, thoughts of blame and self-criticism keep coming to you. You are embraced in feelings of loss and total despondency. But know this: God is with you, even here.

Gradually, ever so gradually you become accustomed to the all-consuming darkness, you cease struggling against it. You simply let it be.

Dimly, at first you *sense*, and than you *see* two signs. The one on the left reads "Death" and there's an arrow pointing down, down some stairs toward shadowy, unresolved hurt and pain. The sign on the right reads "Life" and points to stairs going up toward an inviting light.

You make your choice: You take a deep breath and climb the stairs to Life. God is with you so take your time. At the top there is an open door. Look into the room beyond. What is the first thing you see?

Beloved Friend, what you see is a sacred message from God. He is showing you, perhaps symbolically, some attitude you are to develop and express or some action you are to take. The decision is yours now: whether to enter the room or not.

Is there something or someone you need to forgive? Do you need to do something, to complete something you haven't finished? Is there a message here for you to cease your frantic activities? Perhaps you must learn to focus on the symbolic vision you just received rather than on needless worry.

Be still. Rest and wait for the revelation that is there for you. Be at peace. Simply wait in God's Love. This moment is all that matters. Thank God that He is with you always.

Presently, speak lovingly and firmly with your secret inner self. Explain to this silent self your need for its cooperation with the choice you made when you entered the room at the top of the stairs.

Now, right now, *experience* yourself following the direction you received in your God-given message. You have chosen Life rather than despondency: You are learning a new thing:

Rest and thank God that Spirit is with you.

The activity of Spirit is your Father-Mother-Creator moving through you to manifest His/Her Good in your life and to establish His Kingdom on earth.

Thank You, God, that this is so. Amen.

The last time I, the author, used this meditation, in the room at the top of the stair there was a window through which the Light was shining. Looking, I saw my father in his vegetable garden. He was moving slowly and laboriously, with his cane held firmly in his left hand and his right foot dragging with each step.

I am my father's girl and do not want to let him go, though he left this earth over ten years past, and I am more than three-quarters of a century. I cling to him in my attempts to emulate him by manifesting the same physical disabilities. I cling to him with restless arms and legs. I cling with the pain in my right hand that sometimes makes my writing a scrawl, and recalls the paralysis that forced him to scratch out his name with his left hand. There are medical explanations for both. There is, also, my sheltered yearning to keep the bond intact, no matter what. I adored my father and suffering to prove my father right and good, have followed the path he forged for me. I am my father's daughter, but I have my inner garden to cultivate. *I am my FATHER'S daughter.* I have healing work to do.

Chapter 4

THE MEASURE OF YOUR SELF-ESTEEM

The reason God created man potentially per-
fect and then set him the task of proving it is
found in the mysterious process called self-identifi-
cation.

Charles Fillmore (1)

This chapter could be titled "Becoming Autono-
mous in a Victim Oriented Society." With unlimited information and massive material possessions
as the measuring stick, we are the most advantaged
nation in the world. Still, we often sound like a nation of victims, swapping our individual stories as
though the greatest misfortune would win some coveted trophy. The simple greeting, "How's it going?"
often brings on such a tale of woe, one would think
there were no sun shining, no groceries in the store,

no schools and universities, no ministers and doctors, nothing for which to be thankful.

One day, shortly after having moved to my present neighborhood, I wanted to become acquainted with my surroundings, so I took a walk to a nearby mall. When I sat on a sidewalk bench, a man in his sixties approached and sat next to me. As soon as he had told me his name and that he, too, lived in the area, he said, "I just had my gallbladder removed," and gave me lengthy details of his operation. Thinking that perhaps he had no friends or family to talk with, I listened attentively to the account of what sounded like successful surgery. Then, he continued with a description of his many other ailments, all of which appeared, to him, to be uniquely traumatic. I trust my listening gave him some measure of solace and release.

In contrast, a friend of mine called me on the day she was to have a second hip replacement. A nurse in her doctor's office had forgotten to take her off a blood thinning medication in time, so the surgeon couldn't operate without endangering her life. She was told this as she lay already hooked up with the IV in her hand, in preparation for the operation.

Laughing, she said to me, "My first thought was, 'Should I be mad at this?' Then, 'Naw, why waste the energy?'" Finally, she had surgery one week after the original date. She is grateful she is not an octopus. If she were, she would have more than two hips to replace. Because she treats her personal concerns with humor, she's fun to be around. This woman is not a victim of life.

Denial of health problems or of deep soul needs is not wise. However, it is just as foolish to allow physical or psychological problems to become the primary focus of one's life. Too much concentration on such concerns robs us of vitality, better health and the joy of fulfillment. At one time or another we all have been injured. If we think we are alone, our spiritual progress is hampered because we are closing ourselves off from those who can give us the prayerful support that we need. We all are perfect in the single eye of our Creator and are here to love and help one another. However, our physical bodies do not have to be manifesting perfect health for us to be of service.

Is swapping poor me stories the main topic of discussion between you and your friends? If it is, just stop it. Surely, you can find something more worthy to talk about if you simply open your eyes. Have fun with it. Look around. Discover a subject that is engrossing and optimistic enough to turn a dreary conversation in another direction. For instance, if a friend asks how you are after an illness, probably he wants to know the facts. But have you ever noticed a person's eyes drift when he has heard enough? You can easily shift indifference to interest by telling your friend about the physical progress you are making or by describing some new goal that you're pursuing.

Christ, the Truth, Heals and Transforms

Both physical and psychological healing starts with one's thoughts. Remember, the Creator's strength abounds in your weakness. The Presence of Christ in your soul has the wisdom and the power to heal, to adjust and to establish divine order in every function of your body temple and in every situation of your life. Read that last sentence again, dear Friend, using the pronoun "my" rather than "your." Read it slowly and aloud. It is the Truth.

However, when healing requires more than affirmation and positive thinking, surround yourself with the Christ Presence and listen, listen to your body. Any ailment you find there has something to tell you. Trauma registers in the body and if not transformed, erupts, sooner or later, as illness. Again, the Christ Presence will reveal to you the way of healing, even when the original trauma is captured and solidified at your bone level.

When you are aware of Spirit moving through you to make you whole, you will receive an added blessing. Along with your healing, you become gifted with sufficient wisdom, compassion and courage to assist others in distress. Positive thoughts keep your heart and mind open to the activity of Spirit in others as well as in yourself.

I know this all too well. Years ago I shut the door on someone who was trying to comfort me when I was grieving over a serious loss. In my despondency, I assumed she had come to pry, and I treated her rudely. Later I realized how wrong that assumption had been. I am wiser now. Today, besides having thanked her in Spirit, I'd like to find her and thank her in person. Perhaps, one day, I shall. My honest need, at the time, was for someone who cared and understood. She had opened her heart to Spirit, but I had closed mine. Had I been free, had I trusted the Universe to bring my good to me, I would have recognized her when she came.

Why is it that we refuse help when our happiness requires it? Perhaps it is that some precise need for healing has not surfaced. Circumstances in life have not brought it to our attention. Possibly, we have a vague sense that something is amiss, and we might have prayed earnestly to know what that something is. But until the answer comes, we must remain dedicated to finding it. Rest assured, there is good reason for the delay. Perhaps others who will be affected are not ready. Delay can give greater wisdom and compassion so that, one-day, we will be better prepared for what is to come.

On the other hand, are *you* directly responsible for the delay? Are you, like Adam and Eve, hiding from your God-Self? In some darkened, submerged corner of your psyche, are you seeking shelter by deceiving yourself as well as others and expecting *that* to be your refuge? Well, I have news for you, my Friend. There is no hiding place.

You can become aware of whether or not you are honest with yourself by noticing when you take something personally. Recently, my friend Richard J. Santo, D.C., who is a Natural Healer, told me that my demeanor changed drastically when we talked about my children's father, my ex-husband. I slumped and became smaller in stature. For over forty years, without knowing it, I had continued to take his physical, sexual and psychological abuse personally. I still gave his former consciousness control over my outer posture and demeanor as well as over the inner quality of my self-esteem.

Of course, I can easily use the excuse that counselors and support groups for the abused were not available then as they are today. Besides, I was busy raising the children, but they are in their fifties, now. I can also say that my spiritual teachers taught me the importance of forgiving, of forgetting past unhappiness and of concentrating on the present, all of which I had done and continued to do.

Yes, there were plenty of outer, busy reasons, blinding me to the festering pain of bygone abuse, keeping it closeted away from view. The simple truth is, however, that I just was not ready to cope with those memories in order to heal. God is a great believer in divine order and God was wondrously good, safely withholding events of my transformation until I was prepared to receive. So here it was again, the forgotten past from which I had escaped, conning myself into believing that, with me, everything was all right. Well, what more was required, now? Did I not pray and meditate. Was I not created in God's image-likeness and, therefore, perfect?

Was this intense self-examination never to stop? Surely, I had forgiven my children's father long ago. Did I not still care for the soul of this man with the engaging grin and the charming personality? Had I not felt such love for him that my marriage vows to him still retain a sacredness, today? Had I not prayed for him and held spiritual conversations with him several times since his passing?

Dr. Santo suggested a gestalt exercise in which roles are reversed: I was to take my ex-husband's position and he was to take mine. That evening, by myself, I followed his advice. At first, there was no connection. I believed that long ago, I had done all I could. I was just a breath away from deciding to forget it, when the Spirit of my ex-husband spoke. He told me how dazzled he had been by the indoor plumbing and the electricity in my family's home. He was just a farm boy, well acquainted with the sexual activities of animals and understood no other means of communication between any male and female.

Of course, the wife's role was to care for him, just as his mother had. Yes, he was a mama's boy and he liked it that way. Children were the mother's responsibility, not the father's. He poured out his frustration with my spiritual interests, my artistic abilities and desires. His passion was for car racing, airplanes and bumming around.

No wonder he had acted out as he did. As this communication continued, a great pity welled up in me for this poor man, for this soul that had missed so much of life. My tears were no longer for me; they were for us; they were for him. The dynamics of our long ago time together took on a more inclusive meaning.

That evening, I no longer took the failure of our marriage personally. I realized that I was not a loser. He had been a victim of his surroundings from the moment he was born. Immediately, my spiritual communication with him changed. With no thought on my part, I took on the role of teacher during the gestalt exercise. Furthermore, I perceived the grace of God in action: For the first time, his soul was attentive to mine.

Previously, when my ex-husband had come to my mind, it had been intellectually, rather than compassionately. I had busied myself clearing away the more urgent and obvious limitations that I had accepted from my jealous, manipulative, *well-meaning* mother who, herself, was trapped as an angry victim of an unhappy marriage. Until these filters were scrutinized and removed, I was unaware of a need to reenter the trauma of my unsuccessful marriage. Now, however, on this bone level, the need and I had come face to face. And the victory was mine.

Thank God, the Truth had set me free. My home vibrated with song and dance.

Another illustration of the benefits in not taking things personally was demonstrated to me by a member of my Huntsville, Alabama congregation. During a class, she told us of an acquaintance who had openly insulted her. "But," she said, "I decided not to take it personally."

She concentrated on the situation objectively. With Spirit's guidance she realized that the other woman, who had an unhappy home life, envied her peaceful, loving manner. Quietly and graciously, she took the acquaintance under her care, gave her some uplifting reading material and brought her to church where she could mingle with our loving congregation. My student, her acquaintance and all of us felt abundantly rewarded because of this one member's courage to relate with love and truth, rather than to nourish an intended insult.

Know Who You Are

When you are honest with yourself, you know who you are. You act in self-enhancing rather than self-defeating ways, because deep within, you know that wholeness is your divine heritage. When folks need physical, psychological or spiritual healing and won't admit it to themselves, often their denial is grounded in fear of what they will find. Refusal to face reality can also be motivated by a desire to retain personal power and control. Sooner or later when the condition or situation worsens, fearful or prideful folk feel victimized and singled out for abuse.

How much wiser it is to ask Spirit for help. Simply ask and trust the Universe to draw the right doctor, minister, therapist or friend to you. Then expectantly, diligently, watch until you find that specific person or group of people. Of course, to do this you need to believe yourself worthy of the attention of the Universe. Let me assure you from my personal experiences that you are worthy. You are special. You are the Beloved of God.

We all have evolved from the dust of the ground, from our clay beginnings or if you prefer, from the most infinitesimal universal elements. We have come more literally from these ancient, basic beginnings than some of us care to admit. We could not have done so without the Presence of Spirit moving through us, molding and shaping each one from a rough, shapeless genesis into the precious and unique individual souls within bodies that we are today. How awesome and delightfully reassuring this is. Surely, when you ask, truly ask this loving, all-powerful Spirit for any good thing, you will find that the Universe already is holding your answer in safekeeping, and your request is granted.

Low self-esteem attaches itself to soul injury. It is unsure of God's love and approval. However, separation from God is never entire, and when invited, Spirit will work in and through and around anything. Psychological injury is often subtle in nature, making its roots difficult to trace. An attempt to do this through analytical discussion of past trauma yields only a misleading shallow understanding, because intellectually dredged up memories are biased. The symbology of an authentic spiritual vision, on the other hand, draws forth the conflicted emotions of the original trauma in such a way that they can be accepted, cared for and healed. The process opens the way for underlying, previously captive, spiritual energies to flow forth freely. Although changing the habitual flow of one's energies might seem to be hopeless, it is possible and, of course, making needed changes holds expansive rewards.

What is your perception of yourself? What is your perception of your relationship to the world? How do you perceive your relationship with God and the Kingdom of Heaven?

In spiritual circles, we hear a lot about the single eye or the inner eye. Charles Fillmore, the Christian mystic who co-founded Unity School of Christianity, wrote, "So you who have looked upon the kingdom of heaven as a potentiality to be realized by the power of your word should change your base and see it as it is—a real place already formed, and waiting for you, as a bride adorned for her husband.

"It is here all about you; the knowledge of its presence only awaits the opening of your interior eye, the single eye, as Jesus taught. When you look with this eye your whole body is made full of the light that is neither of the sun nor of the moon, but of the Father."(2)

My mentor in Eidetic Therapy, Dr. Akhter Ahsen, is a student of Western psychology, Eastern philosophy, mythology and religion. He echoes Fillmore's words and expands our understanding of the natural progression of consciousness that occurs as this inner eye opens. He unites spiritual and scientific concepts and, as mentioned in the Preface, he describes the process in detail: The "third mental eye represents the penetrating vision of a unifying consciousness. It is in this mental eye that union, destruction, and regeneration take place. The light in the eye is the manifestation of action, morality, and virtue, a creative force which dialectically breaks, unites, breaks again, and then reunites for revelation of experiential content." (3)

Rather than rationalizing and talking endlessly about psychological handicaps, my students and I find that enlightenment comes clearly, easily and readily when, in the Life Essence, concentration on sacred visions opens the inner eye. It is through such visualization that innate purity changes one's emotional state and, therefore, one's perception of self and others.

The Quality of Your Self-Esteem

How *do* you perceive yourself? In your eyes, are you less than others? Are you more than others? Do the rapid changes we all are encountering, today, appear to you as threatening, challenging or motivating? I hasten to confess that my computer threatened me three days ago when it swallowed this entire chapter.

All of us should care enough for our personal well being to be fully aware of the present quality of our self-esteem. Therefore, in reflecting on and answering the following questions, be fearlessly honest with yourself.

1a. When there is a vigorous disagreement or serious misunderstanding, do you feel guilty until you apologize to the others involved? Do you usually blame yourself for what has happened?

1b. When there is a vigorous disagreement or serious misunderstanding, do you tend to discount and blame the other person or persons involved? Must you always end up being right?

2a. When you are complimented for something you have done well, are you uneasy until you give someone else the credit?

2b. When you are complimented for something well done, do you feel puffed up even though you try not to show it?

3a. Is there someone in whose presence you feel distressed and anxious because he always puts you down? Do you always let him?

3b. Do you feel powerful when you put another person down?

4a. Do you often hesitate to voice your opinion because you're afraid that you might be wrong or that you might hurt someone's feelings? Do you feel compelled to keep the peace?

4b. Do you say what you think, no matter what? Does giving your *honest* opinion often include being rude?

5a. If you are introverted and shy, do you believe that in some ways, perhaps spiritually or morally, you are superior to other people and that they ought to realize how special you are?

5b. If you are an extrovert, do you believe yourself to be more capable and talented than others and, therefore, superior to others?

When you answer "yes" to some of these questions, do you regard your corresponding actions as your duty to God, your humility before God or what? In Micah 6:8, we receive valuable instruction: "And what does the Lord require of you? To act justly and to love mercy and to walk humbly with your God." It is in this way that we ennoble ourselves.

Obviously your "yes" answers point to areas re-
quiring healing. Think seriously about these consecu-
tive suggestions and then, when applicable for your
improved self-esteem, put into practice the related
exercises.

1. When involved in a heated dispute, remove
yourself from the situation as soon as possible. Become mentally and emotionally quiet with the realization that no one is entirely responsible for what
has happened. It takes two or more. Although this
may be difficult if you prefer to control everything,
objectively get all the facts in order. Using paper and
pencil helps. Ask for God's wisdom and discernment
in sorting things out. Believe that God is in the situation and, therefore, only Good can come for all concerned.

Enter the Life Essence of your being, experience
yourself with the other(s) in that situation. Explain
to the other one(s) how you are feeling. Listen for
the response. Then allow God to speak through you
in the vision to mend the relationship. Practice this
experience several times before actually meeting with
the other(s), in fact.

2. When you do anything, Spirit is moving through
you. Giving others all the credit is to imply that God
does not express through you. The opposite is true.
You are created as an expression of God, and an ac-
knowledgment of this and of your Sacred-Self, the
Christ, places the glory where it belongs and empow-
ers the whole situation.

You will not diminish yourself nor will you feel
puffed up if you mean it when you say something
like, "Thank you. I'm thankful it turned out so well."
Then if appropriate, you might want to add, "I re-

ceived lots of help from . . ." Try it. You will feel enormously pleased and humbled.

3. When was the last time someone discounted you or that you put someone else down? Take a moment and experience yourself crawling on your hands and knees to that person from whom you accept intimidation. If, however, you are prone to domineering others rather than empowering them, experience someone crawling to you.

Symbolically, that is what happens when you are fearful of another or make someone else fearful of you for any reason. In the vision, allow your feelings to consume you until you come face to face with how inappropriate your actions and attitudes have been. In both instances, ask God's help as you open to the Truth of Christ within. Behold yourself honoring and empowering the other and yourself until intimidation no longer dwells in either consciousness. Congratulate yourself when the inner experience becomes outer. Also, notice the mysterious, wondrous improvement in your other relationships.

4. Peace is important in any exchange with others. However, first of all peace is an inner attainment. Truth and wisdom, so necessary for growth in consciousness, sometimes promote outer dissension. God is in the situation. God is always with you. In the perception of the Single Eye, there is no right or wrong. Allow Spirit to move within you to express your most sacred thoughts and feelings. If you are in some way mistaken, Spirit will, as the schoolchildren say, "show and tell," and you will learn something. There is no shame or blame.

If you are often rude and communicate without wisdom and consideration for others, start noticing the affect that your words have on you. How do you feel while you are speaking and after you speak? What affect do your words have on others?

"But the wisdom that comes from heaven is first of all pure; then peace-loving, considerate, submissive, full of mercy and good fruit, impartial and sincere"(James 3:17).

Ask Spirit to speak through you with appropriate words of love and wisdom. Envision yourself allowing this to happen, until you find yourself, without hesitation, acting accordingly with friends and family. After all has been resolved, thank God for a Universe that holds you forever in Its love.

5a,b: Whether you are an introvert or an extrovert, you might regard yourself as superior and special. If you do, are you trying to even the score for some sense of loss you have in your life? You never will. Only Life itself can even the score, and then only if you let It balance the scales. Otherwise, your soul will continue to yearn for peace and a feeling of your specialness, but not for your superiority. In your Life Essence you know and want this to be true.

You are, indeed, special, but know *how* you are special. In God's eyes you are pure, the Beloved of God, the Christ. And the Christ is divinely special. When you think and act from your Christ awareness, when you use your talents to the Glory of God rather than for your own aggrandizement, you are, indeed, special. And so it is with everyone. During your next quiet time, contemplate the beauty and the sweetness of Christ.

Self Identification Through Divine Guidance

In Exodus 3:13, God directed Moses to deliver the Israelites out of Egypt. Moses replied, "Suppose I go to the Israelites and say to them, 'The God of your fathers has sent me to you ,' and they ask me, 'What is his name?' Then what shall I tell them?"

God said to Moses, "*I AM WHO I AM* . . . This is my name forever, the name by which I am to be remembered from generation to generation" (Exodus 3:14,15).

It behooves each of us to give careful attention to our use of the words, I am and I AM. The I AM is God's name, the Christ within man and woman, the true spiritual creation whom God made and continues to make in His\Her image-likeness. Are you learning to say with Jesus that "it is the Father, living in me, who is doing his work" (John 14:10)? The I AM also can be explained as the metaphysical name of the spiritual Self, the Self in perfection, the Self that is each one's individual destiny.

Becoming aware of how you identify yourself is paramount to your spiritual growth. Do you know *who* you are, that you are a sacred human being, beloved of God? Do you thankfully accept *where* you are in the evolutionary scheme of things without getting stuck there? And, at the same time, do you believe *in your heart* that your movement toward Oneness with your Creator and with all of Creation is divinely directed?

As an analogy, suppose you are in New York City, seated in your Mitsubishi, packed and ready to drive to Los Angeles. You have already unfolded your map and marked New York City as your starting point. You did not look for Miami on your map and claim that as the beginning of your trip, because if you had, the signposts and the routes would be incorrect, miles out of line. Neither would you look at Los Angeles, your goal, and claim that to be your starting place. On the contrary, you would plan your route along the guidelines on your map starting from New York City. You would follow that route from city to city, over mountain and plain, and you would enjoy all the magnificent scenery and all the places of interest. All along the way, you would accumulate meaningful mementoes, and finally you would reach your destination, Los Angeles.

So it is with your spiritual journey toward Oneness. When you live life fully, you honor where you have been, where you are now and where you are going. You are, as all of us are, born in ignorance and growing in awareness. Coming from such an innocent beginning, without a doubt, has been a trip in itself. You have been carried forward by Spirit, and have accumulated evidence of God's grace all along the way. The awe and wonder of the plan and purpose of it all is mind-boggling. Where and when do men and women reach perfection? In God's eyes, it is right here and right now. There is no time or space; there is no praise or blame with God.

In our limited comprehension, however, the I AM, the God Self is distinguished from the I am, the human, mortal, sensate self. Jesus called the I AM the Father. Most importantly, the I AM is the Father and the giver of the personal will. Our task is to patiently and expectantly establish a conscious unity between the I am and the I AM. Only then are we doing the will of the Father. "Yet not my will, but yours be done" (Luke 22:42). Only then can the Creator work in us and through us. And so it is in divinely guided Self-identification that our individual souls evolve into Oneness.

As we all know, it is a mysterious phenomenon that when we heal one soul injury, often another one of which we were completely unaware emerges. If this happens to you, do not waste time condemning yourself for not being further along your spiritual path than you are. Churches have taught us to resist or ignore our humanity. But discounting the sacred quality of one's joys and trials is like trying to skip all the rungs on a ladder to reach the top. Recall the words of Charles Fillmore, "The reason God created man potentially perfect and then set him the task of proving it is found in the mysterious process called self-identification."(4) How do you identify yourself?

Recently, I have found that accepting and honoring my humanity frees me from resistance to my ever-present good. I have no desire to skip any moment of the happiness *or* the pain with which God has moved me through this wondrous human experience. I no longer hide, ignore or depreciate any situation or relationship that ever has been, is now, or ever will be in my life. Looking through my Creator's eyes, all is Good.

When we yield all our moments to divine wisdom and power, we see that our perfection requires more than intellectual affirmations of our personal goodness.

"Now a man came up to Jesus and asked, 'Teacher, what good thing must I do to get eternal life?'

"'Why do you ask me about what is good?' Jesus replied. 'There is only One who is good. If you want to enter life, obey the commandments'" (Mathew 19:16,17).

All glory goes to the Father-Mother-Creator as Spirit works through us toward the Oneness that we will realize when I am has diminished and I AM is all. The wonder is that when we cherish each human moment as sacred, we find our Heaven right here on earth.

These words I believe for myself. You, dear Friend, must find your own identity. In God's eyes, you and I are both perfect as we are created, right now. Does not the human parent smile at the perfection of the toddler taking her first steps, even when she falls down?

There is a saying, "The higher you go, the stronger the wind." That is so. However, the higher you go, the more spiritual tools you have to work with and the closer you are to God. Life is something of a roller-coaster for all of us. Perceive it as an adventure, as a mystery to be solved according to the rules of the grand universal game. You are created to win because you are worthy of the best, but you will find your best only when you consciously identify yourself with the Most Ancient One, the Lord of all Creation, your God.

Meditation Exercise I

Take a question in this chapter that you have had difficulty resolving. The practice of any of these exercises takes only a moment. Work with the one you have chosen, being sure that the vision originates in your Life Essence rather than your human intellect.

Through the activity of Spirit, the meaning of the Eidetic actually reaches and influences other involved persons. Your Christed Self is where you receive your guidance, healing and fulfillment.

Meditation Exercise II: Releasing Self Blame

Enter the Life Essence. You are surrounded by and enfolded in the love, wisdom and strength of God. The joy you experience is one with the joy of the Universe for you are One with all that is. All of Creation is in your heart.

Begin with your memory of the earliest relationship during which you acted in a way that is no longer acceptable to you. Calmly and without stress, simply ask the involved individual to forgive you for your actions. Let compassion take over the situation.

Spirit knows that you did as well as you knew how at the time. Now you know better.

When the other receives your request, you will know that your present communication is enough. Know, also, that if necessary, your request will linger around and within the other's soul until he/she is willing to respond affirmatively.

Continue this, in sequence, with all toward whom you have acted in ignorance. Let this meditation experience be a release, transforming all obvious or hidden burdens in your soul and, by the Grace of God, encircling you and each and every one of your relationships in love.

Thank You, Father-Mother-Creator, that this is so. Amen

Chapter 5

DO YOU REALLY WANT TO FORGIVE?

"Father, forgive them; for they do not know
what they are doing."

Luke 23:34

Alack of forgiveness is the negative energy that manifests as injustice and violence all over the world. Within this chapter—which is longer than the others—you will find five main sections. I suggest that you move through each section slowly, meditatively and with thorough introspection. Often it is the subtle and hidden attitudes that undermine forgiveness. It is possible to forgive intellectually but to hold onto crumbs of unforgiveness unconsciously.

What is your honest answer to the title question? Do you really want to forgive? If your answer is "yes," what's stopping you? If your answer is "no," what's stopping you?

Does forgiving a certain person or situation seem as senseless and as impossible as changing the course of the Mississippi River would be?

Probably you have heard the statement: If you don't forgive, you're only hurting yourself. Is your response, "It doesn't feel like I'm hurting myself"? Perhaps the snide remarks and the dirty looks you send him make you feel superior. It feels good to be mean to him. You've won, at least for the moment. You don't feel hurt at all and in no way do you think you are *not* hurting him, *not* putting him in his place. Someone's got to do it and it might as well be you.

The disadvantages to such thinking are many. So let's take a more comprehensive look at just who suffers when you condemn someone. If you don't forgive, the *first* person you hurt is yourself because you are separating yourself from God. God loves you and everyone else unconditionally. That is, your Creator condemns no one, holds no grudges. God loves all of His children equally, and that Love is palpable. It is not some emotion you can think or imagine into existence. It already is: God is Love. You know Love through your awareness of God. It follows, of course, that if you close your heart and mind to another, you are turning away from God, who is unlimited Love for all.

Furthermore, Truth is contrary to the platitude that if you don't forgive, you are only hurting yourself. If you don't forgive, you are *not* hurting only yourself. The hostility you send out contaminates the atmosphere around you, contributes to world unrest and universal chaos. Your spoken desire for peace on earth is hypocritical until you strive to care for your neighbor as you do for yourself. Holding a grudge colors everyone involved in the situation with darkness. But most of all, it darkens you and invites more troubles into your life, other people with whom you will find fault and have difficulties. Without a doubt, forgiveness is a primary requisite when we choose to grow spiritually.

There are several twin reasons that make us feel unable or unwilling to forgive with anything but lip service. Fear and anger is one twin reason; criticism and manipulation is another; panic and control, a third. There probably are others, but I trust that as you contemplate these, your mind will expand and your heart will open so that you will pardon any transgressor and move closer to the fulfillment your Creator has for you.

Fear and Anger

Fear and anger are, perhaps, the greatest motivation for refusing to forgive. They also keep us from experiencing our Divinity.

Psychology, today, diminishes or ignores the beneficial activity of Spirit in restoring one's soul and mending broken relationships. Fear ridden, angry victims of childhood abuse—whether physical, psychological or both—come to Centre, asking me for the comfort of communicating with their God. Other professionals with whom they have counseled have insisted that they confront their "toxic" parents who have abused them. These psychologists and psychiatrists agree that confrontation often meets with denial and greater estrangement from the parent. Nevertheless, they rationalize, it will shift the power in the relationship from the parent to the adult child. Thereby, the parental control that has kept their patient a victim, presumably, will be eliminated. As mentioned in Chapter 2, during such confrontation, separation not only becomes greater, but also the one confronting, develops little or no compassion. He remains the victim of his own warped satisfaction in having power and getting even. Apparently forgiveness does not necessarily play a role in open confrontation.

My students and I have a different story to tell. Overt confrontation is not a consideration with us. Clever, cutting remarks are not acceptable, either. According to our experiences, there is a caring, more expansive method that facilitates forgiveness and growth in both parties. Spiritually mature, adult children respect and honor their parents as being worthy of soul healing as much as they, themselves, are.

How merciful are you? Do you care enough to understand that your antagonist—whether relative or acquaintance—is loved by God just as much as you are? Forgiveness is the key. Enter your Life Essence and invite the guidance of your sacred spiritual visions. You will be given a specific method for pardoning any offense, mending any relationship. Sometimes Spirit opens the way for a compassionate outer exchange, sometimes not.

As an illustration, there follows a correspondence, dated 9/20/00, that was sent to me by a dedicated student. She moved to another state after studying Eidetics with me from July 1997 to January 2000.

> Hi Dana,
> This is a quick note to tell you about a miracle. I have been doing a lot more work

on forgiving and letting go of resentments
with regards to my parents. By the end of
July I made it. I had done a lot of writing,
crying, and eidetic work and it paid off. I
truly have forgiven them. It's very freeing. I
find it so much easier to talk with them than
ever before.

So here's the miracle. I wrote a letter to
my Dad to tell him that I love him and to
thank him for all he's done for me and our
family. I also told him that I forgive him and
I asked him to forgive me if I had ever hurt
him in the past. I told him that I knew he
did the best he could.

Well, that was almost six weeks ago. Over
the weekend I received a thank you card
from him, thanking me for the letter that
he enjoyed. He told me that I was a joy to
them and that "We love you very much." I
don't ever remember my father telling me
he loved me. All the pain and suffering
through all this process has paid off beautifully.

There were times when I thought this
wouldn't be possible. But as I have learned
many times, miracles do happen. Here's
another one.

Thank you, Dana, for all your help, guidance and prayers during this (eidetic) process.

Love,

Now, let us consider the deep, perhaps unac-
knowledged, fear that forgiveness will do no good.
The reason you know it will do no good is that you're

sure the other person will never change. That makes you angry, because if you forgive, you will only be hurt again. There is an old saying: "If he does it to you once, shame on him. If he does it to you twice, shame on you." The implication is that you should not allow it a second time, and there seems to be no better way to protect yourself from its happening again than to refuse forgiveness the first time. You need to keep your guard up, don't you?

There is a solution to the dilemma of being required to forgive versus the protective need not to forgive. Would you like to become detached enough from the situation to be happy and peaceful with it? Would you like to have more spiritual wisdom? Would you like to free your mind and, at the same time, be assured that you will not be hurt again in that same way, especially by that same person? Well, you can. And an understanding of the results of forgiving and of not forgiving is a step in the right direction of solving the dilemma.

In *Love Is Letting Go of Fear*, Gerald G. Jampolsky says, "Forgiveness is the vehicle for changing our perceptions and letting go of our fears, condemning judgments and grievances." (1)

To use similar analogy, the lack of forgiveness is the vehicle for anger. When you decide to release your anger, there is no need for a lack of forgiveness, so that vehicle has to go. But how can you fully let go of an emotion that is as strong as anger? If you push it down and refuse to think about it, it erupts in unexpected, inappropriate and destructive ways. So it is with all of us. Why does this happen?

Our basic need for food and shelter is native to the soul. Our basic desire for love and the good things of life is also native to the soul. When our right to pursue and fulfill these needs and desires is denied, we become afraid and angry. Our instinctive shift into a consciousness of fight or flight is automatic.

Today, men and women in the armed services know as much about this as cave men and women knew millions of years ago. So do members of street gangs. However, for most of us, the use of fear and anger has undergone transformation. You and I may not fight against flesh and blood, but we should be taking firm stands against the twisted use of universal Principle and corruption in high places. Do we not fear for our country and feel a rush of adrenaline, of anger when we perceive underhandedness and depravity in our government? Are not these fears and angers given us to signal needed improvements? When our individual awareness has grown to the place where we use our energies with passion and wisdom, when we no longer strike out physically and blindly according to raw impulse and emotion, then we will be following the teachings of the great avatars.

Jesus did not stuff his anger. Although some teachings are that He was too mild mannered for any emotional display, surely there was right (righteous) use of anger when He turned over the tables in the temple. Jesus was not a violent man, because He transmuted the energies underlying fear and anger into a passion for God. His passion was for the movement of the Father through Him, a passion that led him to His resurrection in God. Know this as your guidance, also. Communicate with God. Become passionate for God. Fill your mind with constant thoughts of God. Feel the warmth of God-Love in your heart. Spirit will fill you when you trust your basic needs and desires and look to Spirit to lift these elementary, natural energies Godward.

Right, and to think that, years ago, I almost taught my son to ignore his basic instincts and to stuff his anger. When Geoff was four or five years old, he tried to play with a neighborhood boy whom we will call Bud. Bud was older and a head taller than Geoff and beat him up every time he went out to play. I had told my son that fighting was not an acceptable way to settle arguments. So he often came running home to me with bruised body and raging feelings. My talking to Bud made no impression at all. So I spoke to Bud's mother. She dismissed the problem, saying, "That's just the way my son is." Then I was frustrated and angry. Geoff's tears and rage finally made sense to me. I told him to do whatever he had to do to make Bud stop. He looked at me with wide, tear smudged eyes. Then he ran like a deer, as fast as his little legs could carry him, across the yard. With clenched fists, he yelled, "I'm going to beat you up!" The bully ran away and from then on they were good buddies.

Children often communicate in a survival of the fittest mode. Suppressing their anger and fears is not the way for parents to go. As with any dispute, getting and organizing the facts, first of all, is necessary. After doing that, I had to recognize and loosen my own feelings of exasperation and indignation. Trusting the innate potential in the boys' ability to work things out for themselves was difficult for me, but until I did, nothing constructive occurred in the relationship. Their innate potential was the activity of Spirit in them and between them. Today, Geoff stands by his basic beliefs and quickly pardons any offense.

Proof that it is best to forgive so that chronic anger can go was clearly demonstrated to me by a woman who came to Centre for spiritual counseling. She hated her son-in-law for taking his wife, who was her only daughter, and her grandchild across the country to live. He had been offered a better position there, but according to her, he valued nothing but money and prestige. She and her daughter had always been close, and she believed his actions were a direct attempt to separate her from the family.

I explained to her the wisdom if letting loved ones go. It has been my experience that when we freely let a cherished one go, he always returns. The return need not be geographical. It is possible to live many miles apart while remaining psychologically and spiritually bonded. When we care enough to release, the next time we meet, the renewed relationship is even lovelier and more profound than before. Regretfully, the woman I was counseling could not grasp this concept. Finally, she became terminally ill with a disease that was worsened by stress. She told me she could never forgive her son-in-law and stopped counseling. I have no knowledge of what happened to her. The prognosis was not good. We can't win them all, not in our time. But God can, in Eternity.

I have been unable to locate the written source, but I believe it was Dr. Ernest C. Wilson (1896-1982), beloved Unity minister and prolific author, who gave some sage advice about not clinging to others. "I loose accustomed forms of good when my progress or that of someone else demands it," he said. "I let angels go that archangels may come into my life. I loose my good, hold it gently, free it readily." (2)

Mahatma Gandhi admitted to having had a temper when he was a youth. He said, "I have learnt through bitter experience the one supreme lesson to conserve my anger, and as heat conserved is transmuted into energy, even so our anger controlled can be transmuted into a power which can move the world." (3)

Can we really conserve our anger and transform it into something positive? With Spirit present, we can. See how you feel after you treat the following as an adventure, a quest for Truth that you will not forsake. Using paper and pencil might help.

1. Remove yourself physically and mentally from the next conflict with which you are dealing and settle into a relaxed, comfortable position.

2. Although it might seem threatening to do so, look into your anger; dialogue with it to discover the earliest times you felt that way.

3. Is the intensity of the anger that you feel, today, appropriate for the present circumstance?

4. Why is your anger really there?

5. Are there memories that need to be healed?

6. Have you gathered all the facts you possibly can that are relevant to the current situation? If not, get them.

After you work with this list, objectively organize the facts. Do whatever you can to further clarify and understand your anger and to find the spiritual help you need for healing. After all of this, look again at your feelings.

Silently, in the Life Essence, express your feelings to the other person (s) involved. Hold nothing back. This is an inner experience to sort out and release unwanted fear and anger. Listen for the other's (s') response. Is there room for compassion and understanding with both parties? If the other person refuses to listen, become twice as tall as he is so that you are the authoritative one. If you must become forceful in physical ways to have him listen and understand that you mean business, do so.

For instance, one of my students buried her psychologically abusive father up to his neck and placed adhesive tape over his mouth. She told him he would have to stay there until he started listening and stopped shouting and calling her degrading names. She left him there for a week, until her next eidetic session. By then he had become quite contrite. The humorous experience freed her of fear and anger and graced her with power.

Again, look at your feelings. Can you follow in Mahatma Gandhi's steps, conserve your anger and turn it into something positive? Has your anger been transformed into a passion that has freed the imprisoned part of you so that you can now start to reshape your portion of the world around you? Can your feelings that once would have erupted in anger now motivate you to take your stand rationally and peacefully, doing whatever is necessary to change a negative into a positive situation? Can they? Will they? Perhaps your answer is yes; perhaps it is no. It's not easy, but it is of great importance that you be honest with yourself. Spiritual growth is a lifetime experience. Unless you are truthful, nothing you do is authentic, especially in the realm of forgiveness.

Criticism and Manipulation

It is so easy to criticize and so ego-satisfying to manipulate, that perhaps forgiving is the last thing you want to consider. However, if your desire is to grow spiritually, you will look closely at the five points in this section. Do any of them describe you?

1. Perhaps you are being criticized by someone, and you have not really forgiven him. In turn, perhaps you feel critical and judgmental of that same someone, and you have not forgiven yourself. Criticism can escalate into hatred, suspicion and a host of other negative energies, passed between two persons or two groups of people. Our feelings about differences in others' beliefs, traditions and habits should be shared with God. In so doing, you will always receive your best guidance.

2. Perhaps the difficult relationship is not a two way street with both parties criticizing the other. Perhaps you, alone, are critical. Is there someone with whom you work or live everyday who displays no animosity toward you, but whom you cannot tolerate? Look closely. Is not the fault you find so unbearable in the other, merely reflecting a similar or related fault within yourself?

For instance, if someone talks too much, perhaps you do not talk enough. Try listening and responding to what she is saying, rather than pulling away from her. It might be that someone with whom you are acquainted carries around a cloud of gloom. In such a case, hear what he has to say and then speak the simple Truth. If it is not accepted, be kind and go about your own business unaffected. Changing him is up to him and God, not you.

A young schoolteacher friend of mine and I started sharing some time together: lunch, movies, etc. I soon discovered that my faith in Jesus, God and the Universe was not only discounted, it was met with

animosity. Quickly, my first impulse was to be critical
of her and her habit of laughing or becoming angry
at things I said. Then looking over our conversations,
I realized that she believed I was proselytizing. So I
decided to let God change the way I expressed what
I wanted to say to her.

The next time I might have expressed my faith, I
said, "Oh, well, I better not say that. I know you think
I'm really weird." Shortly after that, we were together
again discussing the fact that violence on TV and in
computer games is corrupting our youth. She asked,
"What do you think about the young people in our
country carrying guns to school and not being allowed to pray in school?" We had a calm, intelligent
discussion and since my views were not as directly
stated as before, she remarked, "I always feel so much
better after talking with you."

"Why do you look at the speck of sawdust in your
brother's eye and pay no attention to the plank in
your own eye? How can you say to your brother, 'Let
me take the speck out of your eye,' when all the
time there is a plank in your own eye? You hypocrite,
first take the plank out of your own eye, and then
you will see clearly to remove the speck from your
brother's eye" (Matthew 7:3-5).

If you had no fault in the relationship, your feelings for him would be those of compassion rather
than blame. You would be doing all you could to help
him.

3. There is a possibility that you are the recipient
of criticism and are doing your best to view the situation objectively. What can you do to find peace of
mind?

If the criticism is intended to be constructive, you
should not ignore it. An explanation might be ap-

propriate as an effort toward a mutual understanding, but long explanations can be fruitless and sound like excuses. Therefore, remaining silent and doing your utmost to view the situation objectively may be the best response. Of course, when you ask God for His wisdom and compassion, these two qualities will add Love to any relationship, a Love that is greater than any human emotion. Mystics teach us to accept praise and blame with the same equanimity, to accept criticism silently and without retaliation even when it is untrue and unjustified.

When such an attitude is God-centered and sincere, rather than an act of pretense at peace while seething inside, destructive energies are wiped out that could, otherwise, escalate into confrontation. Furthermore, you are ennobled when you remain unmoved from your spiritual Center, your God. Leave judgment to God. His is a finer order of living that establishes justice and peace in your relationships and in your world, when you do not interfere.

4. Without being aware of it, you might even try to manipulate circumstances to prove yourself *right* and the other *wrong.* After all, if you're right, there is no reason for you to take the first step toward understanding and forgiving, is there?

One young woman in her thirties admits that she became an attorney so that she could win the heated arguments she still has with her mother. She has come to realize, however, that her ability has become a problem with the rest of her family and her friends. She told me that she is so focused on being right and is so determined to win that no one wants to talk with her anymore. She is studying to change this.

There is a more interesting challenge that she— and you and I—can take. Why not quickly forgive and release little slights so they don't build up? Why not find some point of agreement with the other party, rather than always having to be right?

5. If you want to change your mind about criticism and manipulation and develop the courage to forgive, you can do so. As suggested in the questions and instructions you were given when dealing with fear and anger, it is beneficial to go apart, become objective and get all your facts in order.

Then with your Creator's help, look for the grain of Truth in the criticism. Do you recoil at the suggestion? That grain is usually there. Perhaps, through the critical person God is offering you a different perspective, and your forgiveness and open-mindedness will reveal some attitudes you will want to release or some latent talents you will want to develop. In God's sight, whatever is happening is a blessing. Once you have found the grain of Truth in the criticism, thank God and quickly make whatever adjustment is necessary without any shame or blame toward anyone.

The Reverend Jack D. Kern, a Unity minister and author of the lovely little pamphlet, "An Experiment in Love," teaches an exciting method of eliminating criticism. It has proven workable for hundreds of my students. He instructs us in the non-verbal communication of love toward persons with whom we are having a problem.

He suggests designating a certain period of time—days or weeks—in which you want to see the demonstration of your desire for harmony in a relationship. During this interval, refuse to criticize the other, aloud or silently. Instead, simply send the other unconditional love. Praise the other person whenever you can honestly do so.

Do not get hooked by outer actions. Do not criticize outer actions, just leave them alone. Every time you're tempted to criticize, envision the other enfolded in the Light of God. You can do this, because you know the other is created and loved by God, just as you are. Become objective and persistent in this exercise.

Without attempting to determine what the other should or should not do, once a day, meditate and behold him wholesome and happy. There will follow changes in the relationship, in him, or even more importantly, in you. No longer will you be struggling to forgive.

"The end result," according to Rev. Kern, "is when you try to bless others with light, you find you are standing in the light, too, and you are blessed every bit as much as the one you've tried to help."(4)

Panic and Control

There are those who think they have to be in control all of the time. Conversely, there are those who fear control and hide from it. They give control over to others, even when it rightfully is their own responsibility. Either way, the fear of having control or the fear of not having control can bring on panic; usually, that panic was first felt during some past trauma that needs to be forgiven.

It is easy to recognize the person who is always in control. But we must observe carefully to see that the passive person often has control also, although covertly. And she learns to hold control well enough to quietly, though perhaps momentarily, feel the satisfaction of having the upper hand. Those who languish in illness rather than attempting to improve their health as much as they can, receive at least morsels of the attention that they crave. For instance, during her childhood, one woman was never noticed by her parents unless she was sick. So as an adult, she controlled family plans and worried her husband with her imagined illnesses.

Whether we are outgoing and gregarious or introspective and reserved by nature, we all like to be in control, at least of ourselves. However, with most people, fears experienced during disaster lead to panic. Can you imagine yourself in an airplane crash during which you do not feel panicked because of loss of control? Special training is required for pilots and stewardesses to teach them methods of staying in control and keeping passengers calm.

As Truth students, you and I are learning similar lessons. Trained to be guided by Principle, the God-oriented individual enjoys a healthy command over herself and life's issues. Because of this, she keeps her relationships and environment peaceful and productive, and she influences others to do the same.

Elizabeth, a successful woman who held a responsible position managing the activities of school children, always spent hours preparing for her leadership conferences that were to be attended by teachers and parents. She was a natural leader in a highly responsible position. She knew this but could not understand why, with all the diligence she applied, on the day before any talk or conference for which she was responsible, she panicked.

One day she found the cause of her panic attacks when she remembered the first situation in which she felt out of control. A connection was made with the fact that intimacy frightened her. Along with feelings of being dangerously close, a fear of desertion overwhelmed her with the same intensity that she recalled experiencing long ago when she was a little girl. At that time, her father, whom she adored, suddenly left the family without any explanation or even saying good-bye. Her mother started working as a secretary and was so distracted by her grief and her need to support the family that she had little energy left for her three children. Together with her feelings of rejection from both parents, the woman had developed a huge sense of guilt and insecurity. Perhaps she had done something wrong. Thereafter she saw little of her father who remarried and had another family. Being the eldest of three girls, she felt overwhelmed with responsibility. She had never forgiven her parents.

During several eidetic sessions, she allowed herself to feel the original pain of her father's desertion and her mother's preoccupation. In these inner experiences, she expressed her emotions in the childlike way—weeping and throwing tantrums—that she would have acted out when she was a little girl, had that been allowed.

When her Heavenly Parents (the name she chose for her Father-Mother-Creator) appeared in the Eidetic, it made all the difference. They held her and comforted her, telling her how much they loved her. During subsequent sessions, the Presence of her Heavenly Parents transformed many disturbing childhood memories pertaining to both parents. As fear and panic released their grip, her memory actually was recreated with the Truth of her being. Not that she forgot the facts of her disturbing childhood but that the pain connected with the facts was gone. She knew herself to be the beloved child of her Heavenly Parents and started living accordingly.

As she accepted the shining Truth that God is her true Parent and that she came through her biological parents only for this lifetime, she learned to trust and to value herself. Compassion developed as she learned to understand her biological parents' immaturity and that they had done as well as they knew how at the time. Because of her excellent inner work, she forgave them and gradually her experiences of panic connected with her presentations and moments of intimacy, lessened.

Although her father died before physical reconciliation could be made, she still can communicate with him through Spirit. Today, she and her mother have a mature, loving mother-daughter relationship. They visit with each other often. Spirit always moves through us, in every situation of life, when we open ourselves to its flow.

Finality in Forgiveness

Have you ever tried and tried to forgive someone who has harmed you only to discover that you simply cannot? Corrie ten Boom, in the following true story adapted from *Guideposts* magazine, shows us how to overcome fear and anger and to forgive even when it feels impossible to do so.

Corrie and her sister, Betsie, spent years in concentration camps during World War II.

Corrie watched her cold, emaciated, starving sister slowly die in camp. After the war, Corrie saw clearly that the great need of the people throughout Europe was forgiveness. One day, she had just finished an impassioned talk on forgiveness during a church service in Munich. She had given the congregation a vivid mental picture of God casting their forgiven sins into the ocean. "I believe," she told them, "God then places a sign out there that says, NO FISHING ALLOWED."

As the people were leaving, she saw him—the former SS guard who had stood at the entrance to the shower room in the processing center at Ravensbruck. Stark, cruel memories returned in a rush of terror: the room of mocking men, the shame of walking naked past that particular guard, her sister Betsie's frail naked form ahead of her.

The former guard worked his way through the crowd, toward her. Thrusting out his hand, he said, "A fine message, Fraulein! How good it is to know that, as you say, all our sins are at the bottom of the sea!"

His hand was out, seeking forgiveness, but Corrie did not lift hers in return. She prayed for the Lord to help her and again tried to lift her hand in forgiveness. Her arm did not move. She felt only coldness clutching her heart. But she knew that forgiveness does not start as an emotion; it starts, rather, as a determination to align one's will with God's. "Jesus, help me," she prayed. "I can lift my hand. I can do that much. YOU supply the feeling."

Later she wrote, "And so woodenly, mechanically, I thrust my hand into the one stretched out to me. And as I did, an incredible thing took place. The current started in my shoulder, raced down my arm and sprang into our joined hands. And then this healing warmth seemed to flood my whole being, bringing tears to my eyes."(5)

So it is with us when we cannot forgive in a human way. By seeking the Lord's help, we can pardon the most demonic atrocities, if we truly want to. Our part is to trust the movement of God through us while we go through the actions. Try this with your God, whatever the name might be. Try this and see what the Most Ancient One can do through you.

Three Additional Thoughts

Along with all of the above, there are three thoughts to keep in mind.

1. Remember that the person whom you are trying to forgive has no power to keep your good from you. Of course, you can give him that power by cluttering your mind with thoughts and feelings that have nothing to do with forgiveness. Such a mind must be filled with something, so it clutches fear, anger, criticism and ideas for manipulative control. Such a mind cannot fathom that its good is already there awaiting a receptive consciousness.

Know that your God is a loving God and that this Most Ancient One created the Universe to hold an abundance of good for everyone. All the desires of your heart are there for you when you open your thoughts and feelings to receive Him. Affirm to yourself over and over: Only Good can come of this. Find a tune to fit these words and sing them over and over again. Dance to your song of love and never let it go.

2. Think tolerantly of the other. If you accept her as she is, you will not build up resentment that has to be examined, forgiven and released. Fran, a widow in her fifties, moved into a new neighborhood, next door to her friend Donna, who was also single. She became active in the church her friend attended, only to discover that Donna's attitude toward her changed drastically. She was too busy to go shopping or even have coffee with Fran. She sat on the other side of church and barely spoke to her after service. For two years Donna prayed and attempted to restore the relationship they once had enjoyed. Of course, she made other friends, but she continued to feel hurt and resentful of Donna's avoidance.

Finally she released all her striving and moved to the next county where her son, daughter-in-law and grown grandchildren lived. For months her family had been urging her to do so. No sooner had she left the area than Donna's attitude changed again. She called, asking about the new home and even came to visit. In a flash of wisdom Fran realized, "Donna felt threatened by me when I lived in her neighborhood and attended her church." With this understanding, she welcomed her friend, shortcomings and all.

To accept others as they are is to empower their growth in Spirit. God is forever moving through each of us, taking care of any changes we need to make. When we accept others as they are, we develop wisdom that allows us to love no matter how others act. The wind blows where it will; when we hold no grudges, all comes right.

3. Know that God is in every situation of your life. Remember the example of Corrie ten Boom. Dialogue with God to clarify divine guidance, especially when clarity is needed for forgiveness. Perhaps your answer will come in a dream or in something that you read or that someone says. But come it will.

One of the most beautiful and viable sayings attributed to Jesus is in John 5:19,20: "I tell you the truth, the Son can do nothing by himself; he can do only what he sees his Father doing, because whatever the Father does the Son also does. For the father loves the son and shows him all he does. Yes, to your amazement he will show him even greater things than these."

When you understand that you can do nothing of lasting value on your own, when you decide to do what you see the Father doing through you, only good will come. When you ask your God to fill you with divine Love and to speak words of forgiveness through you, rest assured, that will be done. Thus, critical, unforgiving attitudes are transformed into discernment and wisdom, and finally, into a compassion that results in whatever form of service your compassion takes.

A Guided Meditation: Forgiving

Sit in a comfortable chair or lie down if that won't put you to sleep. Stretch and move a bit to relax. Close your eyes. Your Life Essence now envelops you and infiltrates your mind and emotions.

Settle in the stillness and realize the Presence of your Father-Mother-Creator. Be aware of your true beginnings, of your connection with the earth as well as your connection with Divinity. Be aware that God's Spirit forever moves through it all. Seek God's grace during this meditation. This is a soul transforming meditation on forgiveness.

The one whom you have difficulty forgiving

stands before you now. With an understanding that the eyes are the windows of the soul, look into the other person's eyes. What do you see? Indifference, hatred, resistance, or what? Will the other person look at you at all?

Now take your time. Look through and beyond the negation. Look directly into that person's soul. You will see a little child there. What is the child doing? Notice how the child is dressed. Is he/she alone, sitting in a corner, curled into a fetal position, crying or what? Just what is going on?

You have the wisdom of a mature adult. In the Life Essence everyone has the potential to be a good parent. So you understand children.

Ask this child what she needs to be whole and happy. Spirit within you is communicating with Spirit within this child of your meditation. Give the little one whatever is needed. Play with him, hold him, kiss him and read him a story. Dress her in a new dress and tell her she will never be alone again. Tell her that you love her and will always love her.

Continue in this way until you and the child are comfortable together. This might take several meditation sessions to convince the child. But the preparation is necessary.

When you are ready, release this sacred vision. Take a deep breath.

Now see the other person as the adult standing in front of you again. Look into his eyes. Say to him, "I forgive you." Can you do that? If not, appeal to Jesus, to God, to Universal Spirit or to whatever Divine Entity is meaningful to you. "I cannot forgive this person by myself. But You can forgive him through me. I open myself to Your forgiving Power, Lord."

Use your own words in this communication and
forgiveness will come. This meditation, Dear One,
should be repeated until there is a definite change
in your thoughts and feelings about the other individual. When that moment comes, thank your Creator. Thank Him abundantly for giving you the ability to receive divine healing for yourself, for the other
person and for the entire situation.

Thank You, Father-Mother-God, that this is so.
Amen.

Chapter 6

THE STORY OF RUTH I

"God Bless The Child that's got his own."
Arthur Herzog Jr. and
Billie Holiday (1)

People invariably ask, "What is Eidetics?" An endeavor to translate the essence of an inner spiritual experience for those in one's outer world is even more absurd than trying to give an accurate description of a sunrise and its fleeting influence on the psyche. We all have wished we could do this, but we can't.

So it is that in trying to describe the spiritual counseling I do through Eidetics, I am undertaking the impossible, but here goes, anyway. We could call the process a form of meditation or prayer, although it differs in its approach to the Sacred. Any experience in which we are completely open and honestly communicating with God, Spirit is active. To fully appreciate an encounter with the Creator, one needs to be the participant and experience the Living God for oneself. The possibility of doing so belongs to all of us.

We grasp Truth first in the intellect; then we assimilate it within the soul. Therefore, an intellectual understanding of Eidetics can be a positive step toward acknowledging the activity of Spirit, even though that understanding is without the warmth and depth of the heart-felt experience. In Chapters 6 and 7, a woman's soul is spiritually healed and her Sacred Self is revealed through Eidetic Therapy.

To accept the presence of a wound, to seek out and dig up its roots is to learn what the wound has to teach. A low self-esteem has many darkened aspects crying for exploration. When an individual's childhood circumstances threaten her self-esteem, and she persistently seeks some glimmer of hope that will guide her toward wholeness, that person *will find her way*. This is the story of Ruth who is and was, even as a child, such a person.

When I first met her, Ruth impressed me with her poise, her straight forward attitude and gracious mannerisms. Here is a woman, I thought, who knows who she is. Only when she came to Centre for counseling and progressed spiritually through Eidetics, did I begin to comprehend the immensity of her arduous, determined struggles.

Ruth's Background

Ruth was born and raised during the 1940's in Alabama, the eldest of six African American children. The house in which they and their parents lived was typical of their community. Ruth recalls a log, placed by her daddy, that served as the step onto the porch.

Her father, who had been slow to develop as a child, became an emotionally dysfunctional adult with whom intimacy was a stranger. Education was of primary importance to him. His dogged ambition motivated him to complete his high school education and then to teach his cousins what he had learned. With his GI benefits from WW II, he received his Master's Degree. Loved by everyone in the community, he became an honored hero, principal of the high school, involved in the church and a political activist. Eventually he was fired from his position as principal because of race. An unhappy, duty-driven man, he found neither peace nor comfort unless he was in his classroom teaching or behind his desk.

Consequently, he ignored his wife and children. Always finding something to do away from home, it was as though he rushed in the front door and out the back. During the summer he worked the farm by giving every member of the family a chore and then leaving. His relationship with his family was administrative only. Ruth stated, unemotionally, that he treated his wife and children like the whites treated the blacks.

Friends and acquaintances considered him a humanitarian. Money that Ruth's father earned was given to his cousins and neighbors or toward his political aspirations. He was tight with his immediate family to the extreme that they barely managed, at

times, to survive. Christmastime was sad. Being the
eldest, Ruth saw the pain of the younger children
when they asked their father about wanting something for Christmas like other children had. Their
father reprimanded them, saying that they were supposed to help each other, not ask for more.

Although he gave financial aid to relatives when
they attended college, he never gave a cent to his
own children for their schooling. Be that as it may,
an education held great significance for Ruth's immediate family and, ironically, her father continuously bragged and claimed that his children achieved
greater things than was so. For instance, when Ruth
worked for a medical doctor, he said she was a nurse;
when she received a Bachelor's Degree, he told everyone she had a Master's. Similarly when Ruth's sister lived in Washington, DC, he broadcast the news
that she was writing the president's speeches. And
so it went with the rest of his offspring.

Ruth's mother kept the home warm with what
she had to offer. Her resourceful cooking and her
unconditional love were the two things her husband
could not take away. She could always prepare a tasty
meal no matter how little food they had on hand.
When the children's father complained to her about
them being a burden and not worth having, she replied, "They will never be a burden for me." At one
time she gave all her own money to him, so he would
leave the kids alone.

Of a passive disposition, Ruth's mother let him
walk all over her, but she manipulated circumstances
when she knew she could get away with it. As long as
Ruth could recall, her mother had used her as a go-
between with her father. So it developed that Ruth
grew up weighted with responsibility for her younger

brothers and sisters and for her mother as well. Furthermore, in caring for and attempting to protect her siblings, Ruth did not win their gratitude. Instead, they resented her position in the family.

Ruth told of one day when her daddy had just purchased a used car and wanted to take a trip. She was eight years old. When her parents returned from working in the fields, she had not yet fed and dressed all her siblings. Her father flew into a rage. She knew her mother would not intervene, that she would just look on and say nothing. Keenly disappointed that she had failed in her responsibilities, Ruth told me that she felt "less than," just as she always felt when in her father's presence. Relentlessly throughout those early years he got the best of Ruth, making her want to cry. She longed for her mother to stand up to her father, but she never did.

In the rural South, church revivals were accompanied by a buffet dinner on the church grounds. Ruth's mother was an excellent cook and everyone liked her food. Ruth remembered one incident when her mother wanted to prepare food for a revival, but her daddy did not provide the means. Her mother cooked, anyway, with what little she had on hand. On the church grounds, her father took credit when he became the center of attention by recruiting people to come and eat his wife's good food. Ruth could see that her mother was hurt, but Ruth was doubly hurt. No one knew what had gone on at home. She told me, "We knew mother was putting a box together under the guise of doing it for the kids. But then at the picnic, we kids waited until the others had eaten it." Ruth had had mixed emotions. She had felt pride in her mother's cooking, even pride that her daddy bragged about it. At the same time, she had harbored a deep anger at her father for what seemed, then, to be outright lies and at her mother for being so passive and for misleading the children.

Ruth's Progress

So much for background. In the context of Ruth's story and with her permission, I am sharing two aspects of her progress as she healed her soul wounds, improved her relationship with her parents and strengthened her self-esteem. One aspect involves her father's demands that she constantly engage in chores and never play. The other aspect involves her mother's passive expectancy that Ruth, a child, fulfill the role of an adult.

From a very young age, Ruth stood up to her father because she knew her mother expected her to. So it was that antagonism between the father and daughter took bud and blossomed like a poisonous weed. Ruth wanted to cry out as a child, but who would hear? Tense, stressed and not valued, she had shingles when she was nine years old. I believed that the activity and guidance of Spirit during Eidetic Therapy would transform Ruth's painful memories.

She recounted an early memory from a time when she was nine years old and was wearing a little green dress with a white collar. She wore this little green dress many times in several of her eidetic experiences. She had helped her mother make it. For a little while in this particular vision, she did not have to baby sit her siblings. She was out to have fun. Ruth hopped on a bike and headed for an alley along which cars often traveled. She forgot that drivers usually ignore the stop sign. As she cycled across, an approaching car narrowly missed her—would have hit her had the driver not quickly braked at the sign. Her daddy's oft repeated reprimand, "Get back here! You're shirking your responsibilities!" settled like a dark omen in her mind and heart. It destroyed any hope of having fun. It was confirmation to Ruth that she was not supposed to play.

A year before Ruth shared this memory with me, she had gone to the Florida Keys with some girl-friends to enjoy a long awaited weekend of relaxation. She had barely arrived when a message came from her family that her father had suffered a stroke. She had to return to Cleveland and to her family responsibilities. Confirmation, again, that she had no right to play.

In one of our many approaches to her father's directive that she work and never play, we used, in paraphrase, an Eidetic found on page 75 of Dr. Akhter Ahsen's book, *Psycheye*. Ruth, as a little child, is in a forest with a man monkey that has the head of her father and the body of a monkey with a red behind. Swinging in the trees, chasing each other back and forth, they play silly pranks, laughing and tickling each other. She pulls his tail and he grabs at her legs. (2)

Following this light heartedness, Ruth's daddy appears relaxed and satisfied.

Ruth asks, "What have you found that's so special it can relax you?"

"I found out something about myself that I did not know," Father says. "I found out how much fun it is to have fun."

Practice using this Eidetic yourself, dear Reader,

whenever a relationship with someone seems too stiff. A little humor does wonders.

In the eidetic process, permanent growth is gradual. Positive experiences like this one are repeated again and again by the student. Eventually her memory is created anew and filled with the Truth with which God is now and always has been conceiving her. Her Image Likeness and her Life Essence are One and present her as a joyous, secure, well-rounded and thoroughly nourished child with wholesome parents. To repeat a familiar metaphor: Just as the acorn contains the image of the oak it is to become, every parent and every child contains the shining sacred vision of what that individual's soul is to become. This is not to imply that the facts of the original trauma are forgotten or denied. Rather, in a splendid metamorphosis, the pain of the memory no longer exists. It is as though the injurious event happened to someone unknown.

The student's repeated focus on individual spiritual visions associated with the mother and father fixes the essential growth of the eidetic parents. As their improved characteristics become dependable in the vision, Spirit communicates with the souls of the outer, physical father and mother. They gradually, definitely respond to their unconscious knowing, to their Spirit. And in doing so, they loosen their habitual destructive attitudes. This is illustrated in Chapter 1.

The people in an eidetic vision take on an individuality of their own. No one tells them what to do after the initial circumstance is introduced. Their spontaneous actions and comments develop naturally, at last expressing God's Image Likeness that is in each individual's Life Essence.

To develop this a bit further: God is our Father-Mother-Creator, our true Parent throughout Eternity. Our thinking and feeling natures are like God's twofold nature of Law and Love, also understood as the masculine and feminine aspects of God. God expresses Himself in the physical male and female, in the biological father and mother. In turn, the biological or physical parents influence and mold the thinking and feeling natures of their human children.

My students and I have found that the student's current view of the father usually is reflected in the individual's present thinking, and that the student's current view of the mother usually is reflected in the present feelings. As the father and mother in the vision become more wholesome, the student's thinking and feeling natures become more harmonious and balanced. No longer does the student find that her thoughts tell her to do one thing and her feelings, another.

When was the last time you felt like doing something nice for someone, but your thoughts said, "Yeah, but what's in it for me?" The goal of my spiritual counseling is to bring peace and harmony to the student's thinking/feeling natures. Through this balance God's Love and Wisdom are given expression.

The Legend Of Purna

There is a legend of a young boy in India, named Purna, meaning "complete one." The legend of Purna is steeped in ancient history, and the children are nurtured on legends. These legends pertain to a city known as Sialkot. The children of Gangis Khan dwelled there at one time, and some of its inhabitants, today, are blue eyed and seven feet tall—a powerful, vital heritage. This is a legend of a young boy after whom the city is known.

A youth named Purna was dedicated to his elderly parents who were blind. They had one burning desire: that before they die, they go to all the temples throughout India and visit the gods.

So young Purna placed on his shoulders a bangi, which is a yoke-like contraption, a flexible bamboo pole with a basket on either end. For years, to satisfy their desire, he carried his parents, one in each basket wherever he went. From temple to temple they traveled until they came to the town, Sialkot. Purna was weary and took the pole off his shoulders to rest.

Alongside this town flows a stream, the Stream of Tears, known as Aik. As Purna rested himself, he experienced a great change. So he stood and said to his old parents, "I'm tired of carrying you! I'm sick of it and can do it no longer! I'm leaving. You go your way now and I'll go mine!"

His parents said, "Just tell us what is in front."

Purna answered, "A stream."

His parents said, "Please, just carry us across this stream; then you can go."

So Purna carried them across the Stream of Tears. When they were on the other side, he looked at his parents again.

"I don't know why I felt so mean and said all those cruel things to you," he told them. Then he placed the bangi on his shoulders again and they resumed their journey together.

During one of his conferences, Dr. Akhter Ahsen

told attendees this legend from his home town, Sialkot. He grew up with this legend of Purna.

There comes a juncture in your life—in everyone's life—to pick up and move on, compassionately releasing your parents in the old way that you have known them. Now is the time for you to refuse to carry their burdens any longer. Whatever "wrong" they did, you view differently once you have shed your tears.

You see them anew, as souls that have been freed and you glean, for yourself, whatever good your association with them has given or taught you. You honor them in that you are, in fact, their biological child. More importantly and first of all, you know that the Universe blesses you; you are the Beloved of God, the child that has his own. You must live life in your own way according to your own inner Truth.

A Guided Meditation: Releasing

Relax now. Release your concerns and anxieties. Our Father is doing His work through you. You have been searching for something to fill a hunger, to satisfy a yearning that does not ever go.

You *know* you are a Child of a loving God. You are leaving the house you have been living in. You are seeking a better life, a life without the strife given to you by your biological parents and others in the world. You are seeking life without the strife accepted by you from the world.

You are trudging up a long, dusty hill. On your left is a steep, rocky cliff plunging down to a swiftly flowing river that has formed a deep gorge. On your right is dusty, barren, deserted land as far as you can see.

You are weary; the bag you hold is heavy. It is filled with the hurts and misdeeds of the past, burdens you meant to leave behind. But they are still here for you to carry.

The sun is hot. The hill is steep and seems to never end. The path is narrow and rutted. You are hungry and thirsty. You are sweaty and tired. But this is what you are doing; this is where you are going, carrying your heavy bag.

Now look across the gorge, to the rocky cliff on the other side. Stand still and look. Above the rocks, you see green foliage. You see trees offering their shade, their cool, cool shade. Other trees are heavy with fruit. You see delicate flowers with their hint of color covering the ground. Bolder larger blossoms bloom in clusters.

Even if you could fly, you couldn't reach the beauty there. The bag you carry with its many burdens is heavy, too heavy. The burdens given you by your family and friends are holding you back.

You curse the cares to which you cling. You weep your tears and say your prayers.

Then suddenly you see it. As you approach the top of that steep hill, you see a footbridge spanning the gorge high above the deep, swiftly flowing water. Taking one cautious step at a time, you start to cross that bridge. Halfway to the other side, something happens. You stand in the middle and look down at the swiftly flowing river. It carries all sorts of debris, moving it out of sight, sucking it beneath its rolling, boisterous waves.

You take the burdens from your bag, one by one; and deliberately, drop them. Down, down they go into that river. Watch them as they disappear beneath the turbulent waters. Watch them as they are sucked into their native nothingness.

Now look up, across to the end of the bridge. Take a step toward the garden-like scene in front of you at the other side of the gorge. Take another step and another until you are there, surrounded by the lovely foliage and the cool shade.

You climbed that hill and you crossed that mighty gorge. Cleansed by your tears, transformed by your journey, you are strong enough to leave it all behind. You are courageous enough and wise enough now to do anything.

And behold! Looking into your bag, you see that it is filled with gems of Wisdom and of Truth. You are the Father's child and you have your own.

Thank you, God, that this is so. Thank you God. Amen.

An Eidetic Meditation: Accepting Your Own

Relax now. Take a moment and find a comfortable position.

You are the Beloved Child of God and you know, deep inside, that you have your own. God has a sacred plan for your life. You have dreams and visions.

Your every pore and atom is filled with and surrounded by the Life Essence that is Your Father-Mother-Creator. Here—in this realm of existence—there is no time, there is no space to hinder you in any way. You have only to release your *personal*, human efforts and let the Father do His work through you.

What is your dream? What is your deepest desire? The word, "desire," means "from the stars" or "of Heaven." What is your heavenly desire, your God-given dream?

This dream is being fulfilled right now. In the depths of your awareness, watch God moving through you, accomplishing your heart-felt desire. See yourself living your desire. Take your time. There is no need to hurry. You are enfolded in the Life Essence. You are the Beloved Child; you have your very own.

When you want to release this spiritual experience, do so. Move around a bit to let it go completely.

Just rest now.

Do not hasten this change in your perception, dear One. But when you are ready, see before you a clean white slate. What is the first image you see on that slate? That image, my Friend, is your mental talisman, your assurance that God is fulfilling your dream. Hold it in your mind and on your heart.

Recall it often as you follow your dream. Your dream guides you to its fulfillment. During your lifetime, opportunities will come; doors will be opened by persons known and unknown. Do not hesitate. You have revealed your mind and heart to the Universe. These opportunities and persons are God-sent. You are a child of God and only Good can come.

Thank You, Father-Mother-Creator, that this is so. Amen.

Chapter 7

THE STORY OF RUTH II

The time for weeping has passed at last.
The time for acceptance has come:
The time to pick up and to do what I can
To further reveal my Creator's Grand Plan.

Anonymous

As mentioned before, the only means of understanding and appreciating Eidetics is to experience the process for oneself. Nevertheless, some folks have asked for a couple of chapters giving an explicit account of my use of and the student's progress in Eidetic Therapy. So I have attempted to respond to this request in Chapters 6 and 7. As closely as possible, I have used the words Ruth spoke in relating her visions to me. She had moved into the spiritual state of consciousness necessary for Eidetics, so some of the expressions might seem unusual, fragmented or vague. I want to explain, also, that because of my endeavor to respond to the request, my style of writing changes in Chapters 6 and 7. I trust that my response to the request for greater intellectual understanding and that my change in style will accomplish the purposes that I intended.

Okay, now let's get back to Ruth's story.

Somewhere midway in the eidetic process, there is a definite change in my students' approach to their parents in the vision. Their resentment diminishes and they start perceiving their mothers and fathers as human beings who did as well as they knew how. Ruth's compassion led her to do what she could to help her parents unfold spiritually. With this motivation, her eidetic parents evolve and regress in unpredictable ways during diverse situations. Through it all Ruth's Spirit prods them on; and despite their uneven progress, their overall movement is for healing and wholeness.

Father's Progress

With ease Ruth enters her Life Essence and establishes communication between her father's Spirit and her own. One of the first questions she asks her father is why he brags and lies about his children. He responds, "A lack of satisfaction with myself. I was lying about myself—not about my children—about an extension of myself."

Leaving the vision momentarily, Ruth tells me, "There is no relationship between father and children. We were all *him*. He still is trying to be more of what he wanted to be. Now he can accomplish this only through his children." She explains further that she is experiencing her childhood emotion with the wisdom of an adult. "Even though I am a child," she says, "there is a sense of pity for him." In the vision she is seven.

Again addressing her father, she says, "I appreciate that you are humane and generous, but I need to remind you that you are not that way with your immediate family. I feel sorry for you. You have so much going for you, but not your family."

Her father flies into a rage, "Ain't that a shame! I do so much for you and this is what I get!"

One of the methods an eidetic student learns to use is to change her size in the vision, symbolically expressing the innate, ever present spiritual quality of power. Ruth becomes twice as tall as her father. Now she has the stature of the parent and he, of the child. She moves toward him to strike out with her childhood emotions, but pity holds her back. Father is still raging. "I do everything for you, and you're nothing but a burden."

An argument ensues during which Ruth tells her daddy that everybody outside is fooled, but that the family knows him for what he is, that he can no longer get away with lies to his family.

Ruth told me that for a very short period, her father received therapy for his alcoholism. To support him, she and her mother went also. Her father became angry, allowed no one to continue the sessions and blamed Ruth for telling family stuff that was none of anyone's business. "We children," Ruth said, "went to Daddy to help him, but that made things worse. He said that Mother was lining us children up against him." At that time he was diagnosed as demented.

Everyone has the potential of being a wholesome parent and everyone has the potential of having wholesome parents. These wholesome parents are Ideal Parents that can be found in the Life Essence of one's being, placed there by God. They are the Image-Likeness of God, the Father-Mother-Creator, the Heavenly Parents..

Wanting to help her father in the Eidetic, Ruth tells him to watch and learn what the vision has to teach. She goes to the wholesome Ideal Father and repeats some derogatory gossip about the Ideal Father that she has heard. He admits that he made a mistake, says that he will get help and tell people the truth. He asks the family to accompany him to the therapist's.

Now her eidetic daddy, who has been watching the Ideal Father, walks out saying, "I'm no damn good!"

Ruth explains to him that he is being given a second chance. Then they are all at the therapist's. Daddy talks with the therapist about his understanding of what he has put his family through. The family asks to come with him to his next session. He agrees, adding that he feels whole now and not that they all are against him.

When Ruth asks her daddy to look at life more positively than he has before, he replies that it is too soon. This is the eidetic father saying that he is not ready to do what is being asked. So Ruth compliments him on his interest in community affairs, and together they recall the difficult circumstances of his past.

Her father grew up as the eldest of ten, and no one respected him. His mother was a strict, determined disciplinarian, very conscious of what the community thought about her. She had attended school only through the fourth grade and was a stickler for education.

Ruth's paternal grandfather was a mild, loving man who took care of his wild cousins and, on his deathbed, pledged Ruth's father to take care of *his* cousins also. Now in the spiritual vision, things are clearer to Ruth. She feels empathy for her father and wants to help him and love him through all the feelings he is dealing with.

During a subsequent session Ruth looks into her daddy's eyes and sees that they are anxious and shifting. He is ready to panic. With the understanding that the eyes are the windows of the soul, she delves deeper and sees a little boy with his head down, kicking at a rock. When she asks him what he wants, he says he needs friends who love him as he is. He needs his father who died when he was very young. He needs the strength of his father. He needs his father to deal with his mother who is mean and controlling.

Immediately, the little boy's father (Ruth's paternal grandfather) appears and stoops down to the boy, saying, "I can't be what you want. I can't change things. It will go back further and further into slavery times. Africa. It would be too painful."

Ruth tells him that he has an awareness, an Essence in him in which there is no time or space. This awareness, she explains, knows how to do what is needed. She asks him to please do it. This is the third generation and she tells him that all these bad relationships must stop. To nurture her grandfather, Ruth holds him and caresses him in the vision. Now he, in turn, nurtures the little boy (her father), promising to be strong and to deal with the boy's mother.

"It is working," Ruth tells me. Her father is happy, smiling and his self-esteem is good. She looks into her father's eyes again and they are stable.

"All is forgiven," she tells him. "I see you as God created you."

This pleases her father, but he says, "It took so long for me to get what I wanted from my father."

Ruth responds that time is eternal and that her daddy should accept the wonderful father that *he* is, himself. Father fades away because, he says, the old person is fading away.

Parents' Joint Progress

When Ruth was a tiny child, her mother started teaching her the many chores for which she would be responsible. Ruth felt overwhelmed. She wanted her parents to love and appreciate her just as she was, to let all the kids be just as they were. To protect her siblings, Ruth accepted the blame when they didn't measure up. Her father expected her to be perfect and told her that any mistake she made counted against him. Because of his constant criticism, she always felt like a failure and often thought, "There must be something wrong with me."

In one eidetic vision Ruth tries to reason with her mother and her father about how she feels. They are irrational and refuse to listen to her. She is just a little girl, but she takes on an attitude of mastery and talks to them about Principle. She tells them that children are souls and that they have to start treating their children differently. With this approach, her eidetic parents listen.

To facilitate the process and to see how eidetic

parents are progressing, the student often repeats a situation again and again. With the encouragement of her parents paying attention to what she is saying, Ruth experiences, in a vision, the day her father has just purchased a used car and wants to take a trip. When he and her mother return from the fields, 8 year old Ruth does not have the children, aged from 2 on up, fed and dressed and ready to leave. Ruth tells her parents that she is doing the best she can, that they must be patient.

Her father says, "It's okay."

Her mother speaks up in agreement, "There's no urgency. Like your daddy says, it's okay. Everything is in Divine Order."

Both parents are calm, considerate and understanding. They help Ruth do what needs to be done. In the vision, Ruth thanks them profusely for their change in attitude and spiritual growth.

Whenever it is appropriate, the student verbalizes for the therapist what the symbolism in the vision means to her and how it applies to her own growth and understanding. This part of the session carries special significance, because as the parents in the Eidetic release harmful attitudes and accept their innate wholesomeness, the thoughts and feelings of the student release and accept likewise.

In her interpretation of the above situation, Ruth says that in her memories of him, her father was aggressive, domineering and alone. She is that way, herself, when operating in the intellect and without feelings. Concurrent with the vision, her intellect is relaxing and accepting life as it is, just as her eidetic father is relaxing and accepting life. Her mother's attitude toward her father changes in the vision also. Rather than just remaining passive, she supports her husband by echoing his statement when she says, "It's okay." Relating this to herself Ruth can see that recently she has not been in her intellect alone as much as she used to be; now her feelings can support and influence her thinking.

Mother's Progress

Nevertheless, she always has wanted her mother to come more into her own. Mother's mission still is to be here, and at the same time not to be. She is like two people, one hiding the other. She manipulates in order to function. For instance, she subconsciously creates division between the father and the children. She feels pleased with herself that their children favor her over him.

Ruth remembers when she was in her early twenties and married. Her father and her brothers "got into it." Not wanting to deal with it, Mother lay in her bed, catatonic. She was hardly breathing, and they thought she was dead. As usual they called Ruth, who was pregnant with her first child. She told them to call the paramedics. Later Ruth's mother said to her, "They all got on my nerves and that was my only way of coping."

In a subsequent Eidetic, Ruth and her mother are seated on the stairs, conversing. Mother tells Ruth, "Now is the time. Before was not the time. I'm sorry, Ruth, for using you. There just was no other way."

In the vision Ruth looks into her father's eyes and sees a message there for her mother. The message says, "I want a clean slate. I don't want to deal with your mother's emotions. I don't want to ask for for-giveness."

Mother chuckles and gives a message to Father in return. It is a message of acceptance, not of sarcasm, saying, "I know what is behind that slate."

Ruth's maternal grandmother died when Ruth's mother was seven. She and her sisters bonded at that time and have stayed so close they smother each other. Her mother does not dare do anything without their approval. She does not dare hurt them by coming into her own. They support each other in their misery and together they pass judgment on other members of the family. They all objected when Ruth became spiritually independent of their religious beliefs. While Ruth was studying Eidetics, she also made a name for herself as a spiritual teacher, and her mother's family patronized her.

Expressing her concerns to me, Ruth said, "My own progression has been in proportion as to how I saw them progress. I did not honor myself."

To help in her own progression, she talks to her mother in an eidetic vision. She asks her mother what she would like to do if she had all the freedom in the world. The mother is afraid to say. She sits and smiles as though she is hiding something. Some little thing is in her thoughts, but she cannot say yet. She is not speaking. Ruth senses that Mother wants to be with her, for the two of them to be working together like partners.

Her mother worked at her sister's day care center, and whenever Ruth visited, she drew Ruth aside because she didn't want to share her with her sisters. Although it made Mother feel selfish and guilty, she was pleased when Ruth and her family moved. She would rather have them move than that she should have to share them. Ruth said that her own feelings have been turned off, intimidated because "things were like that."

After she married Ruth found herself copying her mother's passive aggressive behavior. However, Ruth's thoughts were determined to let nothing hold her back and so her feelings just had to go along with her thinking. She said that in this way she was like her father. She perceived that her husband, like her mother, was more passive. But she hastened to explain to me that he was her balance against the disasters in life. She was assertive, go, go, go, push, push, push.

When she was in her late twenties, Ruth thought she wanted her husband to be more aggressive. They had a car accident because she pushed him into a decision. He had said, "No," but she had insisted. She realized that the accident was God's intervention; and as a result, she has learned patience and has worked to release her habit of manipulation. When she told me this her husband had made a decision to return to school. He wanted to get a Master's Degree so that their kids would look up to him.

Parents' Communication Improves

In many eidetic visions during several therapy sessions, Ruth continuously yearns for her parents to be closer, to communicate more with each other. She wants her father to be supportive of her mother, easier to be with so that she (the mother) does not have to visit her sisters to get away from home and the father. In other words, Ruth wants the family to bond.

At one time her mother and her mother's sisters were planning on buying a piece of property so that they could have a garden, a place for the family. They asked Father to join them, but he accused Mother of being unfaithful. Ruth felt helpless and very angry.

Using this situation to move into an Eidetic, Ruth screams at her father and beats on him. He is surprised and shakes it off, although he simmers down some. Ruth's rage continues as she tells him the family will not tolerate his fantasies and accusations anymore. When Father walks off with a "poor me" attitude, Ruth calls after him that she wants to talk with him like an adult. Father says he is open to that.

She looks into Father's eyes and sees that he is rational. When Mother informs him that she wants to buy some property, he does not respond until Ruth instructs him to be whole. Then he says, "I will support it, but I am angry. My manliness is threatened. She is doing something with her sisters and I'm jealous. It's not my idea or my money. Your mother is stepping out of her role, making a decision, and that makes me very uncomfortable."

Mother persists, "Accept something that I am contributing. It's for you, too, and for the family."

Ruth adds, "If you don't accept it, Mother might leave. She doesn't need you anymore."

Father is in shock.

Ruth, sitting in my office, is spaced out. The intensity of her involvement has disoriented her. When something like this happens, the student benefits from experiencing her connection with the earth to help her become grounded again. Ruth takes a moment and breathes deeply. Before we part, Ruth enters the following nature scene from *Psycheye*, by Dr. Akhter Ahsen: "Being in a forest, the earth is moist under your feet and the ground rustles. There are numerous sounds—birds, animals. All sounds are harmonious and blend. The smell is fresh and clean and it seems to rejuvenate you. Relax and enjoy being in the forest." (1)

I pray with my students so that they leave Centre standing on a firm foundation, with an assurance of potential wholeness for everyone with whom they are working.

During a subsequent session, Ruth's eidetic, biological parents are told to watch and to learn from the Ideal Parents as they discuss purchasing some land. The Ideal Mother simply announces that she has plans to purchase some land, and the Ideal Father says, "Good. We will keep the place, and I will use some of my money to keep the place up."

Then, there is the repetition with the biological parents, giving them an opportunity to show what they have learned. Father confesses that he was so messed up he did not see the good life he could have. Now he will cooperate. Mother tells him she knew he had it in him to be cooperative and that is the reason she has hung in there.

Ruth came out of the vision and said, "That purchase of land was a workout."

In describing the meaning that the eidetic vision held for her, she said, "Sometimes like my father, I rest my thinking. Like Mother, my feelings were numb, neutral when I first started this therapy. Now they are just feelings that are not to be ignored."

Changes in the Family Dynamics

Ruth's father did not want the children to bond with each other for fear they would stand against him. It was all right that they bonded with their mother, but there was no way they could bond with their lonely, dictatorial father.

In an eidetic vision Ruth tells her parents that she wants to feel more connected with them. She needs some empathy and understanding of her feelings so that she can interact and not be "acted at." She needs to be treated like a person and not an object. Father is listening. She tells her mother to keep the faith and then what is desired will come. Mother's response is one of hope and cooperative optimism.

Returning to present facts, Ruth has a pain in her side, the right side. She goes inside her body to look around and sees a tissue-like knot that is pulsating. She unties the knot and it's gone. "Surrender, give up, release," she says. "The knot came outside of my body. All those limiting experiences were outside."

Ruth expresses her insight as to the meaning of the symbolism in this vision, saying, "My thinking is still a little caught up in negative things about my father. My feelings are neutral, almost to the point of being unaffected just as Mother is unaffected by Dad now. And I'm getting a real nod from Mother, 'Yes.'"

Throughout her therapy, despite her father's inability to bond, Ruth yearned for intimacy within her family. Her daddy drove family members away, not only with his domineering mind set but also with his social ineptitude and his demeaning, shaming attitude toward them. He called his sisters and his girl children degrading names. He hated his youngest brother and his youngest son, both of whom never finished college. Although one hundred fifty people came to her father's seventieth birthday celebration, not one of his blood relatives cared enough to come. During an eidetic session, Ruth talked with him on a peer level about all of this.

When her father became ill, Ruth had the responsibility of paying the bills and keeping track of the family finances. From his bed and during his recuperation, he tormented her with accusations of stealing his money and lying about it. Their estrangement became so powerful that when Ruth visited her parents, he did not speak to her or challenge her in any way.

Ruth said, "I take that as a positive. I was not dragged down by him." She did not give up with him, either, in Eidetics or when she saw him personally.

Once when Ruth was in the city where her parents lived, her mother called her and asked, "Are you going to come see your dad? Bring the newspapers I left behind. I'll be away."

Although Ruth realized her Mother was manipulating, she went to her parents' house. When she entered and saw no one, she called out, "Is anyone home?"

Dad, who had not been speaking to her, answered, "I'm in here." During the entire visit, he was pleasant and receptive, even communicating with more than a grunt.

When she told me about this, Ruth said that she thought of the visit as she would think about an eidetic experience. There was, she explained, mirror-like meaning in her mother's actions and in her father's new attitude. The way she perceived her father reflected her thinking, in that now he was positive and receptive. The way she perceived her mother reflected her feelings. Ruth saw her mother as manipulative, and she related to her mother and to her own feelings with caution. Mother still regarded Father as a "bad guy" and often telephoned Ruth to relate tales of his misconduct. Ruth wanted to stay focused so that outer opinions would not take over her inner ability to be compassionate and understanding. The excellence with which Ruth likened her consciousness to the happenings in her outer relationships was evidence of her spiritual development.

In an eidetic vision, Ruth declares her freedom by addressing her parents, "Mother and Daddy, I wish you both well. Be at peace. I'm going my way. You will be all right. I have to go on, live my life, do what I can so my kids can be free."

Echoes of the youth, Purna.

The Family Finally Bonds

It was obvious that a change had taken hold of her father when he quieted down in his actual life. He started staying home and did not go to the tavern anymore. Just as remarkably, he continued to get along with Ruth and started communicating with his other children as well.

After her father had a massive stroke that was followed by a stay in the hospital, he was sent home where he remained in a coma for several weeks. He had not opened his eyes, although he had opened his mouth to cough and had moved his legs and his arms. Sometimes he perked up, becoming more alert when a minister-friend came to see him and displaying a spurt of energy when family and friends circled his bed in prayer. Mother silently resisted her husband's oncoming death, but Ruth remained in her calm center, knowing that everything was in good order. His digestive system had failed, and it was just a matter of time.

Ruth remarked to me that it is hard when a person does not know who he or she is. Her mother did agree to go to a geriatric clinic where she could learn to care for herself better. However, Ruth said that she would like her father to have had greater enjoyment and more awareness during his lifetime. Although her father's mother had never nurtured him as a child, his family was nurturing him now. That gave Ruth great satisfaction. "There is an aura," she said, "an energy of my father accepting the nurturing."

On a Tuesday, Mother told Father she would be all right. When Ruth's father actually started to slip away, friends and family circled him, holding hands and praying. Twice, he received energy and came back briefly. Then they just let him be. On Thursday, while Father was passing, a volunteer Hospice nurse told Mother to sing, to keep on singing and to pray the Twenty Third Psalm. Mother knew her husband in the depths of her heart. She also knew what was back of her husband's slate, back of his personality. She called out to him, "There is nothing to fear!"

Ruth sees meaning in the log her daddy placed as a step onto their porch so many years ago. "It is," she told me, "a step from there to here." She has taken that step well. She also has placed a step for her daddy and continues, in Spirit, to enfold him in love.

The eidetic spiritual process is not complete until there is harmony in the student's mind and emotions, until compassion is blossoming in the student's soul. Then the expansion of harmony and compassion continues on for a lifetime.

From her biological father, Ruth said she has received the importance of taking care of her teeth and of proper eating, the value of an education, her determination and her concern for excellence. From her mother she has received her love, compassion and an ability to nurture. In one vision Ruth experienced herself with arms spread wide, embracing the entire world. Today she is an ordained minister, with a widespread congregation made up of all ages. Her prayer is, "God, love difficult people through me." She is well prepared to serve with that responsibility.

A Guided Meditation: Freedom

Relax now. The Spirit of Christ in your soul has wisdom and power to heal and adjust every function of your body temple, to manifest through you all the honorable desires of your heart.

You are in a meadow, lying under the shade of your favorite tree. Watch the white, puffy clouds and the twittering birds, the tiny insects and a squirrel scampering in the tree. How does the ground beneath you feel? Smell the freshness of the earth. Breathe in the fragrant air and listen to the soft breeze whispering through the leaves and grasses.

The sun is shining, not too brightly. It is a perfect day. It's your kind of day: soft, gentle, cool. You doze;

then suddenly you feel some large, rather sparse, raindrops splash on your face and you are awake. If the sun is shining and it is raining, surely there is a rainbow. You look and—there it is—you see the most beautiful rainbow ever. It stretches, magnificently and brightly, from one side of the sky to the other.

You want to climb that rainbow. So you go to one end and start up. By what means do you travel? Do you creep up the rainbow; do you scamper; are there steps for you to climb; is there something mechanical like an elevator for you to go up on? Do you have a sense that your method of climbing reflects some attitude you have toward life?

On what color or colors do you climb to the top? How does the color make you feel? What does it mean to you? Take your time. There is no hurry.

At the top of the rainbow, you pause. You stand and look all around at the blue shaded sky and the soft clouds enfolding you, at the earth below. What do you see on the earth? Again, take your time. How do you feel?

What do you want to do as you stand at the top of your rainbow, looking all around? What is the desire of you heart at this moment? Whatever it is, you are free and you respond to that desire. You do it. You manifest your desire, right now. Take your time. Let this experience be fulfilling. Let it be rejuvenating.

Thank God that there are no limitations on your desires, that all your desires come from God's Desire to fulfill Creation's Grand Plan on earth.

Thank You, God, that this is so. Amen.

Chapter 8

TO STAY OR NOT TO STAY

*But when he asks, he must believe and not
doubt, because he who doubts is like a wave of the
sea, blown and tossed by the wind.*

James 1:6

The Silence is thought of as being the finest and purest connection with God that is possible in our busy world. Surely, the splendor experienced there is unsurpassed. However, something additional is spoken of in 1 Thessalonians 5:16-18: "Be joyful always; pray continually; give thanks in all circumstances, for this is God's will for you in Christ Jesus." Doesn't this mean that you are to communicate with God every moment, no matter what you are doing? How is that possible?

Dearly Beloved, when you know who you are and

where you are—one soul in a garden of souls, all blossoming into Oneness—your relationship with Creation expands. You find yourself in a Garden of Eden before anything is hidden. Through you, humanity is being presented with a second opportunity to remain in the Garden. A longing for your own spiritual growth and your sense of belonging with others adds to your inherent desire to stay.

The discovery that Truth really works excites and inspires you. Awesome spiritual experiences awaken you to new possibilities. Perhaps a deceased relative or friend has communicated with you. Possibly a visitation from Jesus or some other sacred entity has lifted you from sudden disaster or from a long, drawn-out ordeal. You start questioning the universe. Can it be that there is more to living a religious life than attending church and saying, "Thank You, God"? Is it possible that there's more to growing spiritually than the demonstration of your God-given desires?

Once you experience the grace of God moving in and through every situation of your life, you realize that there are, indeed, no coincidences. You realize also that grace is grander than anyone can imagine. You start watching for Spirit's revelations rather than trying to make something happen on your own. You listen and apply Truth with a relaxed, assured and easy manner rather than with exhausting effort.

In such a consciousness you are revisiting the Garden. God is taking care of you, and you feel safe. You do not intend to leave. But, alas, distractions pull you away, and you start to lose sight of Truth. Thereupon, the Garden beckons again: Love is here; God is here; Truth is here. And you cannot stay away.

"If you hold to my teaching, you are really my

disciples. Then you will know the truth and the truth will set you free" (John 8:31, 32).

Such a promise is worth embracing.

What Distractions Make It Difficult to Stay?

Your harmful thoughts, your fears and your learned responses make it difficult to remain in Truth. A few examples of these hindrances follow for your consideration.

1. One fleeting thought that is contrary to Truth banishes you, at least momentarily, from the joy and the splendor of the Kingdom. Excuses are plentiful: What's the point? I'm only human. I'm not walking on water yet, so what does anyone expect? Besides, Jesus lived 2000 years ago, things are different now. Biblical scholars are proving that it's all just a myth.

Any excuse, dear Friend, is the voice of human reasoning. There is an awareness in which purity of thought is possible and in which the highest order of existence is the norm.

2. Are you fascinated with technology and the information highway? Have you been enticed into climbing some corporate ladder—even a religious one—to the degree that your communications with Spirit are superficial? Are you so absorbed with getting recognition and numerous possessions that you ignore the one Source and Cause of your existence? Do you live for self-gratification, for self-glorification? Do you no longer wonder at the mystery and magnificence of Creation?

If so, you have lost your life to something temporal rather than living it for something sacred and everlasting.

3. Many hear the Truth. Are you one who is spiritually oriented in that you attend classes and workshops where you study Principle and learn from someone else how you should apply Principle in your life? Have you soothed your troubled emotions and developed positive self-esteem? Do you contemplate your needs and desires, choose your goals, imagine their fruition and affirm your good? Do you put forth great human effort, rushing around to achieve objectives, attaining an almost god-like ability to manipulate circumstances and even life itself?

All too quickly, work for personal gain becomes laborious. If this is your experience, it would be wise to ask yourself how much you worship your personal consciousness and discount the Giver.

4. Have you learned to enter the Silence? Do you believe the Silence to be the one unencumbered path to the Garden, the only means of pure communication with the Almighty? The Silence is luminous and transforming, but does it unite you or separate you from others? Do you take the peace and love you receive during the Silence out into the world? Jesus did. Mother Teresa did. Paramahansa Yogananda did. There are others who did. Do you? Or do you come to the Garden alone and experience unspeakable Oneness only until some voice of woe says that you must go?

Why must you go from the Garden? Do you want to martyr yourself to prove your worth as a good person? Do you create your own suffering, thinking that suffering will make you like Jesus? My Friend, the crucifixion of Jesus happened once, establishing an apex in the evolutionary progress of men and women. It doesn't have to happen again and again.

Without the crucifixion, there would have been

no resurrection to demonstrate the new consciousness which you and I, even now, are moving into. Jesus' life teaches and shows the inner way, not the outer way of transformation. Your challenges hold a special message for you and focusing on God, rather than on the difficulty, will bring about your personal metamorphosis.

When you accept the sacred message given by Jesus' life on earth, you understand that as humanity develops—or more personally, as you live according to Principle—you will not suffer in the way it is perceived that Jesus did. Jesus' message is not one of martyrdom. It is one of a love for others and of a faith in God that will lift you from all your earthly woes. Jesus exemplified this Truth throughout His life on earth and, most especially, during His crucifixion. When you arise from the Silence because the voice of Love calls you forth, you will serve God and His entire Creation. Mother Teresa did not serve the poor in order to save herself through the personal poverty and suffering that she experienced. She served because of her boundless love for God and humanity.

5. Mother Theresa surely had moments of Silence, and she surely remained centered in Christ all through each day. But when the Silence is regarded as the only path to God, I am reminded of a question that came to my mind over twenty-five years ago. What of the people who are so busy fulfilling their God-given responsibilities that they have no time to enter the Silence with methods which they have been taught?

A woman in her mid-twenties came to my office for spiritual counseling. In her arms she held a large sleeping baby with angelic features and an oversized

head. She explained that the child was not only
Mongoloid but had been blind from birth. She was
troubled by what she had heard during a class on
meditation. The instructor had emphasized the need
to sit in a certain chair, located in a certain quiet
place, at a certain time every day. The teacher said
that other attempts at meditation were undisciplined
and would not lead to the coveted Silence.

With a stifled voice this mother told me about
her daily activities. She arose early to feed and dress
the baby and her three year old. Then she bundled
them both in the car and took the older child to a
day care center. For the baby's safety she either held
the little one or kept her within sight every moment.
She told me that her husband worked two jobs to
pay the medical bills. When he came home at two
o'clock in the morning, she arose to spend some time
alone with him while the children were safely sleeping.

Weeping softly, she said, "There's no time for me
to meditate. I feel forsaken, like God doesn't love
me."

When I asked if she ever thought about God, she
brightened. "Oh, yes," she said, "all the time. Especially when the baby is taking her afternoon nap and
I do the dishes. There's a window over my sink and I
can look out into the garden. I talk to God then."

"That," I assured her, "is meditation. You have
your moments of Silence."

Is Continual Communication with God Possible?

Somewhere along our evolutionary path, men
and women have come to believe that humans are
not good enough to be fully aware of God every

moment. But that is not the Truth. Especially today, our communication with God can and must continue beyond the moments that are commonly accepted as the Silence.

Throughout our recent history, many who have proclaimed and acted on Truth have not been tolerated by the authorities or, sometimes, by their peers. But they persisted. Anne Hutchinson (1591-1643), along with her husband and fourteen children, was excommunicated from the Church and banished from the Massachusetts Bay Colony. She had attacked the claim of the clergy that they alone heard the voice of God and that redemption came through deeds rather than through faith. Bernadette of Lourdes (1844-1879) was burned at the stake because she insisted her guidance came directly from God. More currently, Martin Luther King, Jr. (1929-1968) and Mahatma Gandhi (1869-1948) both were shot to death because they lived the Truth that was written on their hearts and souls. Although they may have had moments of inner turmoil, surely their minds and hearts did not entertain separation and doubts regarding their Creator for very long.

When you pray, when you enter the Silence, do you wonder why *you* have to leave God there when the time comes to arise and continue your day? Please know, my Friend, you can take God with you. Nothing delights me more than to meet others along the way who know that this sacred relationship can be unbroken. Such joy to experience this Oneness and to know that it is more than simply desirable: It is possible.

Twenty-four years ago, Gerald G. Jampolsky, M.D., founded the first Center for Attitudinal Healing in Tiburon, California. In his most recent edition of

Teach Only Love, he says, "Personally, my mind and heart have undergone a deep shift since I wrote the first edition of *Teach Only Love.* My relationship with God is now beyond 'belief.' I find that I am listening and talking with God all day long. You might say that my day is filled with God talk. My journey from atheist to absolute faith in God required me to forgive certain aspects of my religious training and a few of my early teachers who did not appear to 'walk their talk' as well as my own misperceptions of God. Today I do my best to make all decisions based on listening to the inner voice of God and to make my will one with God's will." (1)

In spite of what you have come to believe about your inability to connect with the Spirit that is God, Spirit is always present. It is the activity of God that is always right where you are. Whether you are aware of it or not, Spirit is here, there and everywhere ready to communicate with you.

Today Jesus and His New Testament followers are being called mythological characters. Some Bible scholars waste their energy in intellectual argument trying to prove the Scriptures false. They talk as though facts accumulated today are the criteria with which to prove or disprove God and the purity of Jesus. But facts are twisted and often contradictory. Rest assured, dear One, Our Creator has not left us desolate. He has prepared another field of consciousness for us where Truth, in spite of words and facts, is known.

Spirit was active during both Old and New Testament times and is active today. Exactly *how* is not for human consciousness to prove. When the intellect ignores Spirit, it is wearing blinders and, despite all its research and arguments, remains ignorant of humanity's true potential. Wisdom gleans intuitively, rather than just intellectually, the sacred messages revealed through ancient as well as modern men and women.

Staying in the Garden Today

We are living in a new millennium now and are surrounded by spectacular progress in science and technology. Besides space travel, one of the most far reaching of these is the World Wide Web connecting all of humanity. As with all innovations, these advances can be misused by unscrupulous human minds. Never has humanity needed to accept the movement of Spirit in its progress more than now. If we do not listen and learn from Spirit, great disasters are sure to befall all of creation, including those individuals endeavoring to improve life with nothing more than intellectual and material progress.

During this evolutionary period, we need a balance between science and spirituality. We need to develop an intellectual understanding that supports Spirit so that we can work with God in the handling of scientific and technological discoveries. We have much information and knowledge on our hands and in our minds, but we need to *know* Truth. Do you, Friend, understand the difference between knowledge and *knowing?* Do you see how the two are created to work together, forming an amalgam of expression and manifestation that we have never considered possible?

The brilliant work of Pierre Tielhard de Chardin affirms a synthesis of all things, both scientific and the spiritual. Psi researchers, such as Dean Radin who is quoted in Chapter 2, are proving the sameness and the blending of these two philosophies, once thought to be diametrically opposed.

In the work I have done with my mentors and in the work my students have done with me, we find that Truth comes intuitively through both our thoughts and our feelings. That is to say that Truth comes through both the masculine (thinking) and the feminine (feeling) aspects of our consciousness. Science is often regarded as masculine and religion as feminine. We can realize global peace only to the extent that our thinking/ feeling natures and our scientific/spiritual philosophies find a balance that is in tune with the Infinite.

Fashioned from the earth, we yearn for union with our beginnings for that is where the Truth awaits our acceptance. The Spirit of God, continually speaking the Word, has molded the raw beginnings from whence we came into the individuals that we are now. Knowing this is assurance that Spirit's unceasing activity will continue into our bright and shining future. Our responsibility is to watch and to let that activity be accomplished through our collective consciousness. Then we can receive enduring solutions to today's global questions and beneficial guidance for today's mysterious universal circumstances.

How does all this relate to you? Your heart-felt motivation, based on good attitudes toward yourself and others, includes justice, compassion, love and respect, all of which travel full circle. In trusting this Law of giving and receiving, you come to grasp the sacred unity of all creatures—indeed, of all Creation. You find that your Oneness sends you yearning for all the earth and all the Universe to benefit from your attitudes and actions.

Do you understand, dearly Beloved, that you can send Spirit forth to break down the inertia caused by fear and disbelief? On the wings of your thoughts and emotions, you can open new avenues of demonstration for your own and for humanity's good.

This is to say that our global society is experiencing great trauma that can be lifted into a glorious transformation by the liaison of all masculine and feminine aspects of nature and philosophy. For instance, as you and I mature in Spirit, our personal masculine and feminine natures are learning to express as one. As within, so without. It follows that we have only to cease viewing science and religion in dire conflict for these two philosophies to move from separation into a productive synthesis. It is not necessary to obliterate either or to subject one to the other. Separation, caused by contrasting the two, is futile. Are not science and spirituality searching for answers to the same mystery, only using different paths and terminology?

One wonders how we can fail to see that which is so desperately needed. Spirit is calling us to display our caring connection with all that is material and immaterial, with all that is animate and inanimate. Our evolutionary growth is crying out for the compassionate embrace of all the peoples of the earth, a loving embrace leading to further manifestation and glorification of Creation.

During 1886, the Statue of Liberty was unveiled and we, in the United States, opened our hearts to everyone on earth. In words and symbols, we spoke our welcome, willing to become the melting pot of the world. In the main entrance to her pedestal, Lady Liberty beckons immigrants:

"Give me your tired, your poor,
Your huddled masses yearning to breathe free,
Your wretched refuse of your teeming shore,
Send these, the homeless, tempest-tost to me.
I lift my lamp beside the golden door!"

Emma Lazarus (2)

We decided on a matter, and it has been established for us. The homeless, the tempest tossed are here now. We are here now. From the Native American Indian to the latest refugee dreaming of naturalization, we face the unformed future together.

A longing for intimacy clings to us, an echo of our true beginnings that aeons ago held us all in one loving embrace. Divine Spirit in me longs to communicate with Divine Spirit in you. We have never needed to be aware of the activity of Spirit in our individual and collective lives as much as we do now.

Thus the spiritual focus, today, is on lifting our individual and collective consciousness. Science claims that it has determined most of the basic laws underlying its disciplines and does not dispute that one of its exceptions is determining the nature of consciousness. Can it be that this divine mystery is to be *experienced* rather than determined—a word suggesting the use of human intellect and will? When our spiritually perceptive qualities awaken, we will find that human knowledge and words are inadequate. One shining eternal moment we will *be* the nature of consciousness. We will know even as we are fully known, because we will experience everlasting Oneness with the Most Ancient Consciousness, with the pristine Law and Love that is the Creator.

Meditation Exercise: Your Path of Service

Just relax, now. You are free to let this meditation flow as it will. As you image yourself, understand that the experience is metaphysical. It will manifest in the world, according to your present consciousness and ability, but it *will* manifest. You will find your unique path of service; thus you will be fulfilled.

Picture yourself, experience yourself as active in the world. There is no time; there is no space. You are in a quantum field: in the world, but not of the world. You are feeding the hungry, nursing and healing the ill in body, comforting the sick of soul. By your actions, you are teaching Love and Truth.

You draw all the peoples of the earth together, joining hands and singing, "Let There Be Peace on Earth" and/or "I'd Like to Teach the World to Sing." Take your time with this meditation. Allow the experience to develop on its own. Let it unfold slowly until your love of God and humanity fills you with overflowing joy.

Thank You, Father-Mother-Creator. Thank You God, that this is so. Amen.

Chapter 9

DECIDING TO STAY

Forget the former things; do not dwell on the past.
See, I am doing a new thing!
Now it springs up; do you not perceive it?
I am making a new way in the desert and streams
in the wasteland.

Isaiah 43: 18,19

You've decided that you *do* want to stay in the Garden where you're motivated by love for God and all of humanity. But sometimes you question whether or not you can measure up. There's a strange discontent in you that demands your conscious decision to stay, but what makes you think you're ready for such a commitment? Intellectually you agree with every word of Truth, but you're finding something unexpected and discouraging. Old habits of thinking and feeling that you thought were long gone are resurfacing, still in need of healing. Maybe Principle doesn't work for you, after all.

My Friend, whenever you make a sacred decision to do a new thing, you are deciding to stay in the Garden. Whenever you determine to forget the former things and refuse to dwell on the past, you are deciding to stay in the Garden. Sometimes it's not easy, but always knowing that God is with you keeps you focused on Him and open to His guidance.

Perhaps you have tried and tried to release a certain painful memory. It might, even today, cause you to hold back in fear of being hurt again. Furthermore, you might not be fully aware of the reason for your fear and hesitancy. Buried deep in your unconscious, past trauma may be blocking your feelings of confidence and security so that your Good remains just out of reach. Perhaps you have been in therapy or spiritual counseling for years, but the need for healing still gnaws quietly and persistently. You struggle to understand why.

As I've mentioned before, one Bible verse that has sustained me through difficult and confusing experiences is Jeremiah 33:3:

> Call to me and I will answer you and
> will tell you great and unsearchable things
> you do not know.

Continue to call; call for a lifetime, if need be. Whenever you call, you are staying in the Garden. Whenever you listen, you are staying in the Garden. Whenever you respond according to God's guidance, you are staying in the Garden. Be assured that your healing is on its way.

It's Only the Beginning

When you make a conscious decision to follow God's guidance no matter what, your understanding of Truth has just begun. You make the decision because you know that if you listen and follow your inner guidance, which is the Truth of Christ, your life with God will be much improved over your life without God.

God is a loving God. He holds no grudges, so rather than dwelling on your shortcomings, recall the times when you have chosen your path according to Truth. If feelings of self-depreciation creep in, they separate you from your identity as a child of God. Change your focus. You have Principle to guide you and a responsibility to put that guidance into practice. Mystically, just the right person or persons will appear to walk with you, sharing the love, wisdom and courage to keep your consciousness pure.

Today, the Spirit of God is undeniably active throughout our entire global society. There are individuals, groups and opportunities that may or may not be directly connected with your established church but through which you can find answers to your particular spiritual needs. Spirit carries the Word of God where it wills, bringing harmony and wholeness to wounded souls and distressed bodies.

The Word of God is the most enduring thing there is. And the Word is Love. Jesus, who is Love, the Word made visible, said, "Heaven and earth will pass away, but my words will never pass away." (Matthew 24:35). Jesus also said, in John 16:26,27, that He will not pray the Father for you, for the Father loves you for yourself. What other proof do you need to communicate freely with God?

Why should receiving Love be a difficult choice to make? When you look with your inner spiritual eye, you perceive the Word of God written on your heart every moment of the day. When you listen, you hear God speak to you. Align your awareness with a moment by moment openness to this inner voice of Truth. Align your will with God's Good, and your challenges will be resolved quickly.

Principle or divine Law would seem cold were it not accompanied by Love, the feminine, nurturing aspect of God. Welcome the warmth of God's Love until its splendor sends your heart soaring to accept and to love others. The time comes in your spiritual growth when you must look outward into the soul of things as well as inward for your own personal soul development. "No one has ever seen God; but if we love one another, God lives in us and his love is made complete in us" (1 John 4:12).

Looking into the soul of a friend calls for more than a ritualistic affirmation about perceiving the Christ in her. For instance, when you and I become acquainted, it should be with the desire to enhance the nobility and sacredness of one another. To love a person honestly and compassionately, right where that individual is in consciousness, opens the way for Spirit to speak to Spirit and awaken insights within both.

You've Been There All Along

During their life experiences in the Garden, Spirit told Adam and Eve the way to declare the Kingdom of God as their own. They decided not to follow Truth. But unlike the mythical first couple, you have struggled enough on your own, and you want to stay in the Garden. So it follows that as your perception deepens, you grasp intellectually that " . . . the Kingdom of God is within you" (Luke 17:21) and has been within you all along. Before now you were only partially aware; you had not made the decision. Now you are through hiding. With cautious determination, you are ready to commit yourself. Just what does that mean for you, anyway?

Commitment to stay in the Garden and to acknowledge the Kingdom within is commitment to let God's will be done on earth. For starters wouldn't you have to perceive God in all of Creation and know that all of it is Good, just as He proclaimed in the beginning? Wouldn't you have to understand that His great abundance belongs to everyone and everything? Jesus teaches us to pray, " . . . your kingdom come, your will be done on earth as it is in heaven" (Mathew 6:10).

At one time the disciples criticized Jesus for allowing a woman to pour costly perfume over his body. "This perfume," they complained, "could have been sold at a high price and the money given to the poor" (Matthew 26:9).

Jesus responded, "The poor you will always have with you" (Matthew 26:11).

This raises a question. How do you reconcile this statement with His prayer in Matthew 6:10 for God's will to be done on earth? Surely, Jesus would not have prayed for heaven on earth were it not possible.

Does it follow then that when you are in Heaven, the poor will be with you even there? Are you to believe that it is God's will for some souls in Heaven to be materially poor throughout eternity?

I think not. However, I am convinced that as long as you believe that God's will *cannot* be done on earth as it is in Heaven, the poor are with you—*you* are the poor. You are poor due to your limited thoughts and feelings, including the thought that poverty is here to stay. It is the poor in consciousness to whom Jesus was and still is speaking.

The poor in consciousness always think in terms of money and materiality, rather than in the Truth of God's abundance. As soon as you realize that there is enough of everything for everybody, you will have and hold riches beyond your imaginings. Jesus made a new stream of thought for you to follow, a new way in the desert of your soul.

A woman in one of my congregations, whom we will call Doris, learned this and received greater answers to her prayers than she had hoped for. She came to my office and said she had three prayer requests. First, she needed a new place to live, because she could no longer afford the rent she was paying. She had applied for an apartment in a Government Housing Development for Seniors several weeks previously, but she still did not have one. Ellen, a friend whom she told of the housing development, had applied there also and had been given an apartment within a week.

Second, Doris hadn't seen her son, her daughter-in-law or her grandchildren for three years. Several weeks before, she had asked our Prayer Group to pray that she would receive enough money for a train trip to visit them during the coming Christmas season. The funds hadn't come, and she was considering calling her son to ask him for the money but said she was too proud to "beg." Just before coming to see me, Doris had been talking with Ellen on the phone, and guess what! Ellen, who saw her grown children and grandchildren every year at Christmas time, said that her son already had sent her an airplane ticket for that year's holiday visit.

Doris' final "request" came as a complaint. "I'm mad at God," she said. "I'm sick and tired of praying. Every time I ask God for something, He gives it to Ellen!"

The Universe knows not to give to a closed heart. As we talked and prayed together, Doris began to understand that her jealousy toward Ellen was making her bitter and, therefore, unable to think rationally. We compared her need to wait for her prayers to be answered with Noah's need to send a dove out again and again, until finally it returned with a leaf, signifying the nearness of land. She came to regard Ellen's good fortune, rather than being an affront to her, as being like Noah's bird returning with a leaf. It was a sign that her own answers were very near.

Thinking more calmly and clearly, Doris called the manager of the apartment building and asked why she hadn't heard anything, although Ellen had received an apartment immediately. After a momentary silence while the manager looked for the file, Doris let out a whoop of delight, thanked the manager profusely and hung up. Someone, she told me, had misplaced her name. There was an apartment waiting for her, and she could move in anytime. Doris hardly could contain herself. We thanked God and parted.

A week later she called, still ecstatic. "You'll never guess what's happening! My son and his wife and my two grandchildren are coming *here* to spend all of Christmas week with me!"

God's Loving Law of Destruction and Creation

As Doris discovered, men and women are subject to both the positive and negative aspects of life, to the Law of Destruction and Creation. This Principle is recognized in all religions. For instance, it is represented by the Hindu god Shiva, and it is expressed in Christianity by the crucifixion and resurrection. It is also confirmed by science. From a scientific standpoint, something is always burned away in the creation of any synthesis.

When you and I, as individuals, are living Truth as well as we can, we sometimes experience what seems to be the burning away of one belief to make way for a new and better approach to living. Today we are involved in a cultural synthesis as thousands of immigrants come to the United States and merge with our society. Reminiscent of our forbears, they are leaving their homelands behind in search of freedom. At the same time we, the established citizens of our country, are releasing useless, often prejudicial thoughts and feelings. We are opening our hearts and minds to the beauty and value of these newcomers' positive beliefs and traditions. For every false or outdated concept released, another Truth is accepted. In that awareness, we will receive yet another challenge to see and to accept an even grander, more expansive Truth. This evolutionary process is for us as individuals, as a country and as a world.

A Guatimalian friend of mine paints homes during the day. When he is off work, he voluntarily teaches Bible to Latino prisoners, men who have had difficulty adapting to our ways. There is no one else who will minister to them. He told me that, whether painting or preaching, he was thinking of God every moment.

Does such dedication seem impossible for you? Does your work, your schooling or your family demand one hundred percent of your attention? Dear One, when you are willing to earnestly seek Him, your gaze will be fixed Godward. You will see and hear Him in all that is, like a melody that stays with you and will not leave. Right now, start to think God, God, God, and soon you will have that awareness humming in the back of your mind. With such a consciousness, outwardly you can be involved in a meeting, a conversation or whatever. Simultaneously, Spirit will be present and will speak Truth through you. You will be amazed and delighted at what you hear yourself saying.

It is possible to ignore Spirit and to call yourself an atheist, but you cannot remove yourself from Spirit. Spirit is beyond human control or comprehension. For instance, you and I cannot anticipate the words or the actions of such persons as the Dalai Lama and Sai Baba. Their lives demonstrate that "The wind blows wherever it pleases. You hear its sound, but you cannot tell where it comes from or where it is going. So it is with everyone born of the Spirit" (John 3:8). There is security in knowing your divine heritage and accepting the will of your Creator as your own.

Jesus speaks to people today as clearly as He spoke to those of His own time when He said, "Yet a time is coming and has now come when the true worshippers will worship the Father in spirit and truth, for they are the kind of worshipers the Father seeks. God is spirit, and his worshipers must worship in spirit and in truth" (John 4:23,24).

However, that's easily said. Even with repeated prayer and concentration on God, it's difficult to overcome some deeply imbedded habits. You might want to respond to certain situations in a positive way, but your reaction seems to be triggered by something beyond your control. Furthermore, Spirit seems unconcerned and unreachable. An unspoken belief comes again and again to your mind that people or situations other than yourself are at fault. You have prayed and prayed, and you simply cannot change what you *do*.

Coping With Learned Reactions

Certain learned reactions contribute to this belief. Case studies are filled with grown people who claim that they can't be good parents or mates because their own parents did not teach them how. One abusive parent said, "Every child needs to be hurt. It makes the kid strong."

From the beginning of human comprehension, it has been expected that the mistakes of parents will be passed on to their children. " . . . I, the Lord your God, am a jealous God, punishing the children for the sin of the fathers to the third and fourth generation . . ." (Exodus 20:5). That has been a fact in the past; today things can be better. We know that we have used this excuse long enough. It is no longer the Truth, it is nothing but a learned reaction.

The Truth is that even little children want to contribute to a life of love and harmony. In a Family Welfare report, a second grade little girl left a note, "I love you, Mommy," before she ran away from home to escape her drunken mother's beatings.

As mentioned briefly in Chapter 3, I once was an assistant to a Prison Chaplain in Lansing, Michigan. While there I counseled a lifer, a man who admitted killing another man. Like all of us, he yearned to have meaning in his life. He wanted me to understand him and why he did what he had done. The first time I realized this was when this prisoner explained to me the *good reasons* he had for killing. I have long forgotten his reasons, but I will long remember his desire to do "good" and have some meaning in his depraved life.

Probably his reaction when he killed was a learned reaction. His behavior patterns didn't recognize any other way of dealing with that particular situation. How do you deal with your learned reactions? Deep-seated habits cannot be changed through the power of the intellect and\or the personal will alone. In such instances, no matter how hard you try and no matter the eloquence of your affirmations, you can't accomplish what you want without something more.

From the time of your childhood, you have been taught acceptable ways of thinking, feeling and behaving. The repetition of these ways establishes deep paths taken by the neurons in your brain until your reactions to life are deeply embedded. They flow as naturally and persistently as the Mississippi River progresses within its banks. Human nature seems to accept whatever works as being okay. But just suppose that what once worked with your parents and childhood teachers, no longer accomplishes what you need and want today.

For centuries medical science has believed that neurological paths in the brain could not be changed. When a neuron was established, that was it. Once a neuron died, that was it. Furthermore, the function carried out by that particular neuron was gone forever. Nothing could be done to change the course of that function or to grow another neuron to serve in place of the old. However! According to recent television documentaries, science is now proving that neurons in the brain can be stimulated to grow again, often along different routes as a person establishes new habits. You can, with practice and exercise, change habits that you do not want and learn new ways of doing things. Even the chemicals in the brain can be changed by repeating an affirmation that is followed by corresponding action. What other proof do you need to strengthen your resolve to do so?

Years ago, a family friend who was a missionary in China, was afraid of heights. There were Warlords approaching the small mission where she lived. The only way she could escape their route was over a long footbridge crossing a deep ravine. Because she knew God supported her, she started across and she reached the other side. With God's help, she did it. From then on her obsessive fear of heights was gone. Without a clue as to what was happening biologically, she was changing the neurons and the chemicals in her brain.

We all can do this. An old habit or attitude might seem as deeply entrenched as the Mississippi, but we can change the course of that neuron, that river in our brain. One person I counseled loved chocolate. Whenever she shopped for groceries, she could not resist buying and devouring a pound box of the candy all in one sitting. After hearing about the possibility of changing the flow of the neurons in her brain, she started envisioning herself changing the course of the Mississippi River. And the river was flowing with chocolate. Very soon she found that by thinking the word, "Mississippi," she could easily walk right past the boxes of candy when she went grocery shopping. Her habit was broken. She was doing a new thing. The old riverbed was gone. She had made a new way in the desert; a new stream coursed through the wasteland of her soul.

Every time you make a sacred decision to do a new thing, you are deciding to stay in the Garden. Watch your thoughts and feelings closely so that nothing detrimental escapes your notice. You may stumble again and again, but again and again visions will guide you, whispered words will comfort you, the right teacher will lift you and stand by you. You will receive the encouragement you need to accomplish the will of the Father.

You and I are the earth-formed Spirit of God. We are destined to reveal the mystery to which we have been drawn from our beginnings and to find that we, ourselves, are the mystery, the shining, divine potential, the perfection that is our Father-Mother-Creator.

The Kingdom Is Within

While revisiting the Garden, you learn to trust Truth, and you make your decision to claim the Kingdom for your home. The Bible teaches many Truths. Be alert and take them to heart as you progress in consciousness enough to do so.

During the Last Supper, Jesus foresaw His crucifixion and symbolically gave His body to His disciples, charging them and all of us to love God and humanity as He did. In John 2:22, the disciples recalled that He had referred to His body as the temple that would be destroyed and raised again in three days.

Jesus gave His body to humanity because men and women always have related to physical sacrifice. Jesus did not mutilate His body. Martyrs in the past, such as some of Jesus' disciples, have chosen to give up their bodies to the will of their oppressors in order to emulate Jesus, His crucifixion and resurrection. Some mystics throughout the ages have injured and mortified their bodies and, because of their self-inflicted suffering, have drawn closer to God. Today, former hostages tell us that they were able to survive confinement and torture only because of their increased awareness of God.

Recently, a focus on keeping one's body healthy and physically pure is bringing new interest and understanding to the statement in 1 Corinthians 6: 19-20, "Do you not know that your body is a temple of the Holy Spirit, who is in you, whom you have received from God? You are not your own; you were bought at a price. Therefore honor God with your body."

We are in a different era of spiritual development now and are choosing to respect our bodies. We exercise and are learning to eat healthy food. Today in our desire for spiritual growth, we see no value in self-inflicted suffering. On the contrary, we strive to keep our bodies strong, healthy and *pure*, fit for service to God in Self and in one another. All we need do is cleanse our consciousness and change destructive physical habits. When thus redeemed, our bodies truly are worthy of being temples of the Living God. And it follows that each person's temple is with that individual wherever he goes.

Church buildings provide a place for the coming together of like minds to share spiritual insights and encouragement. Joined together inside or outside of a building, all spiritually minded individuals are the body of Christ, the body of Truth. However, the physical *experience* of Truth can be known powerfully in one's individual body temple. Today we need to cherish and take good care of the body so that while we are in this physical form, we can create our own Heaven on earth.

When you decide to cling to a consciousness of Love and Truth and to live according to Principle, you are deciding to stay in the Garden. But do you understand the meaning of "The kingdom of heaven is near" (Matthew 10:7)? When you *experience* the Kingdom, you see that it is just as Jesus said, " . . . the kingdom of God is within you" (Luke17: 21). The light of the body temple is the spiritual eye. When your joy is to serve God and humanity, you find that no effort is necessary in doing God's will.

How splendidly Dr. Akhter Ahsen combines the physical and the mystical: "The circle of the iris, with the pupil at its center, feeds the fire of the psyche in man, but his third mental eye represents the penetrating vision of a unifying consciousness." (1)

It is your physical, human perception of yourself, of your world and of your Creator that determines your psychic relationships with self and others. It is your spiritual sight that manifests your sacred unity

with God, with all of humanity and that fulfills the
two greatest commandments of the Law.

Jesus was asked, "Teacher, which is the greatest
commandment in the Law?" He replied: " 'Love the
Lord your God with all your heart and with all your
soul and with all your mind.' This is the first and
greatest commandment. And the second is like it:
'Love your neighbor as yourself.' All the Law and
the Prophets hang on these two commandments"
(Matthew 22: 36-40).

Meditation Exercise: Doing the New Thing

Take a moment now and center yourself. Release
your personal thoughts and feelings. Your personal
thoughts and feelings may be mistaken. God is never
mistaken. Acknowledge His Presence throughout
this entire exercise.

The Life Essence of your being is your soul's home.
You are comfortable here where there is no time, no
space; where there is only God. Except, there is something—a learned habit or attitude—you have tried
to get rid of, but can't. When pressured it erupts,
gushing forth completely out of control.

Right now, this very moment, remember the Mississippi River. Tune in to its surging rhythm, in to the
power of its symbolism. You are about to stop the old
flow of your thinking and feeling and to form a new
path, another neuron in your brain. You are about
to make a new way in the desert of your soul, a new
stream in the wasteland of your mind.

Envision yourself using whatever equipment the
Universe gives you, closing off a raging, destructive
Mississippi River, the devastation of your habitual

wrongdoing. You are digging a new pathway for the direction of wholesome, clear waters.

Take your time with this, dear Heart. Repeat this exercise once a day. It takes only a moment, so enjoy it. Feel the power of your God-given transforming energies.

Whenever you are tempted to slip back into your old habit, think "Mississippi" and follow through with your new-found ability to do the better thing.

Thank You, Father-Mother-Creator for the power of sacred vision.

Thank You, God. Amen.

Chapter 10

FOR HIS GREATER GLORY

*"In the same way, let your light shine before
men that they may see your good deeds and praise
your Father in heaven."*

Matthew 5:16

Do you let your light shine or do you curse the
darkness? Do others see your accomplishments
and praise your Father in Heaven? Or does fear of
failure stop you from realizing your dreams? Perhaps
the opposite is true, and determination to make a
name for yourself leads you astray? Another question: Are you so cleared of human disbelief that you
"'Love the Lord, Your God with all your heart and
with all your soul and with all your mind'" (Matthew
22:37). Jesus taught that love for God is the first com-

mandment. "And the second," He said, "is like it: 'Love your neighbor as yourself'" (Matthew 22:39).

The surest way to master life's great lessons is to live according to these two commandments. Such mastery would be impossible were you to rely only on human love and understanding. Even common ordinary decency would be impossible were it not for the spark of Goodness and Truth burning within you. This spark is the Christ-Light, a spiritual fire that is constantly burning away the old and making way for the new. The energy of its flame reduces to less than ashes all that is unloving. Simultaneously, it shapes and solidifies a love so innocent, so pure that you know again your shame-free beginnings. An awareness of and an alignment with such a Light is desperately needed in our world.

The ultimate purpose in *Revisiting the Garden* is to awaken you, dear Reader, to the constant activity of Spirit in your life. With Spirit shining through you, your light will never fail. Your thinking, your feeling and all of your senses will welcome alignment with His will and you will dwell in His Kingdom right here on earth. So watch and listen. His will for you is His Word for you, and His Word for you is written on your receptive heart.

What will you do after reading this book, my Friend? Will you put it on a shelf and let that be it? If you are honest and your answer is, "Yes," I implore you to reconsider. Surely, whatever insight and inspiration you received while contemplating these chapters requires more than that. Nothing beneficial will be gained if you forget this visit. If you do not measure your experiences in the Garden against your old understanding and then put your new found Truths into practice, your time will have been wasted.

The Most Ancient One demands nothing of you now or ever. But your yearning *will ever hound* you until you accept His Love. There is no need for you to be "perfect" in order to connect with God. The only thing received from rushing around and forcing what you perceive to be your perfection is spiritual indigestion.

Therefore, I suggest that you simply do what you can with relaxed persistence and dedication. Act on the desire that led you to pick this book up in the first place. Make what was your *intention* to grow spiritually, a *reality.* God is not too far away geographically to touch you and to heal you. Hold on to your lofty vision. God is not too exalted and too removed in consciousness to speak to you with unconditional Love. He knows where you are and He hears your cry. He will meet your heartfelt need even though you may be in your darkest hour, surrounded by depravity and corruption.

In the words of Paramahansa Yogananda, Founder of Self-Realization Fellowship, "I want to teach you that God is your own: dearer than the dearest, nearer than the nearest, more loving than all things that we love. If you would but treat Him that way! If you would but lift one hand, He would drop two hands to lift you up. If you are unceasing in grasping for the hand of Spirit, He will come without fail."(1)

To assist you in grasping God's hand, there follow ten reminders of the essential meaning in each chapter of *Revisiting the Garden*. Remember, there is no need to accomplish everything at once. If you unwittingly fail one of life's lessons, another opportunity surely will come your way. In Truth, with an awareness of Spirit, you cannot fail.

A Summary of Essential Points

1. *Nurture your desire to change.* Envision yourself as the new person. Pray deeply and express your gratitude for Spirit's activity in your life. You will reach the time when, through God, your troubled past is of no consequence and your destructive habits dissolve into nothingness. In Chapter 1, Greg's consuming desire to control his temper so he could be a good husband and father was realized because of his diligence in communicating with Spirit. Today he has a loving wife and family and is using his talents to serve humanity and to glorify God.

Give your desire for change to God. When you relax in God and decree your Good, your transformation will be sure.

2. *Awaken to the activity of Spirit in your life.* Spirit is all around you and within you. The very breath you breathe *is* Spirit. Spirit is pure energy and is ready to function on your behalf if you let It. Enter your Life Essence often. You will feel Spirit close to you there and you will see with God's sight that everything is blessed.

Of course, you can worship in churches, temples, mosques and cathedrals all over the world. But no special structure, location or religious ritual is required to worship God and no personal method of devotion is deemed unworthy. Many who have survived concentration camps and others who have been hostages or prisoners of conscience have stories to tell about their personal awakening during starvation and torture.

Charles Fillmore, American mystic, tells us that it is our "privilege to rise out of this plane onto the spiritual plane and thereby come into open communion with the Father and know as Jesus knew and have all the powers that He had—and greater ones."(2)

This spiritual plane is the quantum field, the Life Essence where there is no time or space, where Spirit moves freely through you, establishing His will in any and all circumstances.

Awaken, my Friend, awaken. Spirit is active in *your* life wherever you are.

3. *Choose to live.* You could be without one dime to your name, enduring hunger, filth, torture and prison shackles, still Spirit would be there. Firm up your intention to pursue God; He is the very best friend you have. When you call He will answer.

Does it seem difficult to make the connection by yourself? Remember the story of Terry Anderson in Chapter 3. His spiritual connection started with his reliance on a Bible tossed into his cell by a prison guard. God's Word, as spoken through Old Testament prophets and New Testament apostles, kept his mind focused on God and on Jesus' teachings. If there is anything that is sacred, if there is anything that whispers Truth, if there is any glimmer of Love, think on these things, my Friend.

You and I have a subconscious and a conscious faith in God. Although it is naturally present in our Life Essence, our faith is formed also on the foundation of our ancestors' evolving beliefs. These forbears from whom we inherit so much, include the first male and female living in the Garden. They include the ancients of all cultures whose inspired insights were taught orally long before they were written down. And they include the predecessors whom you and I remember: our parents, grandparents and great grandparents. Their tranformative experiences live in our consciousness as surely as their DNA lives in our body cells. Their wisdom is ours to cherish, to prayerfully consider and to intelligently apply in life today. The Truth of Christ in everyone is both innate and acquired.

Find the Truth of Christ for yourself, honor it and never let it go. Choose to live.

4. *Know who your are.* Allow no person, place or thing to take away your identity, your divine heritage. You are the Child, the Image-Likeness of the Creator. There is no way that you could have emerged from your inscrutable beginnings, no way you could have become the wondrous creation that you are today without the movement of Spirit within and all around you.

Throughout your past evolutionary growth, your unconscious relationship with the Most Ancient One has brought you to this apex in your everlasting Life. Somewhere along the way, you became conscious of your self and of God as separate entities. Now you know the Truth: You are emerging from the Ageless Consciousness that has been, is now and forever will be.

With this awareness, you are spiritually hungry in every aspect of your being. You are becoming more God-like with every prayer and with every manifestation of Principle. Oh, how you love the mystery with which God does wondrous things through you!

You, my Friend, are the Beloved Offspring of Almighty God. Know this to be True.

5. *Forgive. Forgive. Forgive.* Learn to hold no grudge against any person, place or thing. When the disciples saw a man who had been blind from birth, they asked who had sinned—the man or his parents. In John 9:3, Jesus answered, "Neither this man nor his parents sinned, but this happened so that the work of God might be displayed in his life." How can anyone fail to grasp this message?

When you commit yourself to staying in the Kingdom, you are making a pledge to blame no one for anything: not your parents or teachers, not your friends or your superiors, not even yourself. Instead of looking for who is at fault, change your focus. What is God doing?

The words of Jesus say it all: "Father, forgive them, for they do not know what they are doing" (Luke 23:34). When you cannot forgive, ask Him to forgive through you. That's all that's necessary. Reread the experience of Corrie ten Boom in Chapter 5 and let it be that simple and that final. Allow God's never failing unconditional Love to so captivate your mind and heart that you cannot tolerate attitudes of criticism and blame.

Forgive and you will be free to make plain the movement of God in your life.

6. *Honor yourself. You are God's Child; therefore, you have your very own.* You know that you have your own, don't you, Friend? Never forget that you are the Beloved Child of a rich and lavish Father. All He has, even all He is, is yours. Allow nothing to remove you from the purity of your sacred Self, from the Truth of who you are.

If the family into which you were born harmed you in some way, seek inspired methods and spiritually-minded professionals to guide you in your healing. By growing wiser than your wounds, you rise above them. Transform your soul by completely forgiving whoever hurt you in the first place.

Ask, dearly Beloved, and you will receive. You are

being offered your own inner strength and guidance, right now.

7. *God is your life.* Your tears are not your life. Weep your tears, but allow them to dry. *Insist* that they dry. There is far too much beauty to let negative memories or unhappy circumstances become the focus for your life. Look around, see the needs of others. Develop compassion. Understand that loving God means loving others. Serving God means serving others.

Know that your Heavenly Parents love you and understand you completely, regardless of any temptation or failure. When you ask for divine help in transforming your weaknesses into strength, God will respond. Let your love of God be strong and let it be known by the way you live your life. Love the unlovely.

As related in Chapters 6 and 7, Ruth honored her noblest thoughts and feelings. She followed her inner guidance to help her parents in their spiritual growth, rather than trying to "get even" with them. In this way the compassion and unconditional love that she developed prepared her for her life-work as a Christian minister.

Today, Ruth reaches many people with Truth teachings—many that no one could have imagined anyone reaching before the advent of the World Wide Web. There is no limitation to the number of persons who read her messages, attend her services and receive her counseling. Jesus said to His disciples, "I tell you the truth, anyone who has faith in me will do what I have been doing. He will do even greater things" (John 14:12).

Let your focus be on God. He is your Life, your reason for living.

8. *Communicate directly and honestly with God.* Dia-

logue with Him about where you are in your spiritual growth. With no shame or resistance, stay close to your Father-Mother-Creator. Speak freely from your heart. Tell Him all your doubts and fears.

Studying the Scriptures can be a means of keeping focused on Jesus and of applying His teachings to your life. Yet as strengthening and lovely as the Scriptures are, they were written at another time by other people.

God is and always has been present for everyone and will communicate with anyone who chooses to go to Him. In John 5:39, is not Jesus scolding some of us? He says, "You diligently study the Scriptures because you think that by them you possess eternal life. These are the Scriptures that testify about me, yet you refuse to come to me to have life."

Speak directly and honestly to God. Remember that God and Jesus are One, so if you find yourself communing with Jesus or some other embodiment of God, it's all the same, my Friend.

9. *Love is all there is.* Make your commitment to stay in the Garden with a new understanding of freedom and with such love for your Creator that you serve Him by serving others. Know that, during this lifetime, you can make your own heaven or hell right here on earth. Establish yourself in Truth by purifying your thoughts and feelings, by perceiving God within and all around you and by loving your neighbor as yourself.

Manifest God's Kingdom in your world by doing nothing of yourself, by doing only what the Father does through you. God is Love and Love is all there is.

10. *Release your selfish ego.* In Luke 1:50, 51, we read, "His mercy extends to those who fear (respect, are in awe of) him, from generation to generation.

He has performed mighty deeds with his arm; he has scattered those who are proud in their inmost thoughts." (Words in the above parenthesis are the author's.)

Once you decide to stay in the Kingdom, do everything to the glory of God. You can succeed at anything by applying universal principle, but scrutinize your motivation. Does it please you to imagine yourself controlling situations and people regardless of *their* desires? Good humored competition can be exciting, energizing and fun, but willfulness and personal pride eventually are followed by a fall. In other words, a vain imagination surely will lead you astray and banish you from the Kingdom. Use your energies, always, to God's glory by living a life that teaches Truth to others. Through your example you will help prepare everyone you meet for the Kingdom and everything you do will have eternal value.

The Lord's Prayer decrees, "Our Father in heaven, hallowed be your name, your kingdom come, your will be done on earth as it is in heaven" (Matthew 6:9,10).

Let this be your sacred vision. It was never meant to be just words.

Releasing Self-absorption

To accomplish all of this, it is necessary to release misleading cultural beliefs, especially those that promote individual and collective self-absorption. For instance, an underlying attitude prevails in our society that, with science and technology, nothing is impossible. A belief that we can establish a righteous kingdom here on earth without much help from God defies the proven Laws of Creation. Pseudo spirituality tries to be but is no compensation for unlimited reliance on human devices. Guidance received from crystals, stars and authentic psychics can partially answer some social and psychological needs. But it falls short of touching the sacred connection we can have with our Creator. It is good advice to go to God first and to the outer as God directs.

Only the application of Principle and reliance on God will give us the peace on earth that we dream and sing about. Without alignment with God's unconditional Love and Wisdom, science and technology go amuck. So do religion, politics, industry and all human endeavors.

Every person is a vital part of the body of Christ. What men and women call good or evil exists, potentially, in everything. Evil expresses as selfishness and greed; good expresses as love, compassion, wisdom and an active concern for all of Creation. Selfishness and greed slacken the progress of God's Divine Plan for the individual and for humanity. Love, compassion, wisdom and service contribute to the healing of men and women everywhere and, therefore, to the resurrection of humanity from the cross of the Universal Christ.

Once upon a time, according to Genesis 11: 1-9, everyone on earth spoke one language. Some people migrated toward the East and settled on a plain in the land of Shinar. There they made plans. "Come, let us build ourselves a city, with a tower that reaches to the heavens, so that we may make a name for ourselves and not be scattered over the face of the whole earth" (Genesis 11:4).

Have you noticed that when a group of folks are doing something "to make a name for themselves," they eventually start arguing? Perhaps their problems are never resolved because they become bitter and part company. That's what happened to our early ancestors in the plain of Shinar.

They needed a deeper motivation, a more sacred purpose than self-aggrandizement. In order to settle their differences peacefully, they needed to speak with Love, to act according to Principle and to praise God. Instead, they worked to satisfy their own ego, developed a limited understanding of one another and spoke in several self-centered languages. No one was listening to anyone else, so they couldn't figure out what they wanted as a group. Despite their plans to stay together, they were scattered all over the world.

It is possible to do some things without an awareness of God, but anything with lasting, positive influence requires the spiritual connection. For example, there are ministers on television who have continued to inspire viewers with Truth for years. They not only speak Truth, they live Truth. Spirit is active. But we are all aware of some televangelists who seemed to start their careers in good faith, only to put aside and forget their original intention to glorify God rather than themselves. Eventually their towers have crumbled in disgrace and anguish. It is easy, when serving others, to be swayed by money, power and the admiration of followers. The crucial point is that when Spirit is forgotten, decisions are made and situations appear that are completely out of alignment with the plan of the One Who knows All and is All.

Mortal plans are scattered over the earth like so much dust or as my first Truth teachers often said, "Mortal plans return to their native nothingness." Our all too human televangelists started to lose their way,

I am sure, by using small discrepancies to manipulate circumstances. Eventually their little slip-ups numbed their sensitivities and became accustomed habits, attitudes and actions that separated them from God.

Condoning small discrepancies in yourself is a mistake because small discrepancies *will* become large. Blinders will cover your spiritual sight and you will find that you are laboring all by yourself. Notice, dear One, how stressful you become when God is not in your activities. Notice how easily your body becomes ill when you are pressured and worried, and there is no help. When totally absorbed with personal concerns, you cannot see God's benevolent plan for your life. You lose sight of your true identity and of your true reason for living.

Furthermore, my Friend, every time your selfishness causes you to harm someone else, you harm yourself. You are a reflection of that person and that person is a reflection of you. Both you and that person are, individually, a vital part of the great Body of Christ, the Body of Truth. Every time you wound yourself or another person, you crucify Jesus Christ all over again. Of course the reverse is valid also. Every time you are a blessing to another, you are a blessing to Christ. "I tell you the truth, whatever you did for one of the least of these brothers of mine, you did for me" (Matthew 25:40).

Today, we live in a new millennium. That we can contribute to health or injury in someone else's body and soul by unwittingly sharing positive and negative psychic energies, was not even thought of until recently. We are learning a new thing.

Let us look again at this stanza from Dr. Akhter Ahsen's, *Manhunt in the Desert*. The message is clear:

The tradition of teaching
By word of mouth is over.
This time He will teach not orally
But physically.
This time He will not offer
Words or symbols in place of Man,
But Man himself.
This time
The Book shall be written
On the body of Man. (3)

There is a Divine Plan for your life. During these exciting times, there are things for you to do that no one else can do quite as well as you. And you will do them well, my Friend, providing you endeavor to remain in the quantum field where you do nothing that Spirit does not do through you.

Find What You Love to Do and Do It

The mythologist, Joseph Campbell (1904-1987), advised us to follow our joy. It's excellent advice, but I recall a period in my life when I thought I could not pursue my personal desires. The responsibility of raising two children left me little time to develop my own talents. Nevertheless, during the years I was alone with them, I must have made an attempt at being a serious writer because some of my articles were sold to national magazines. The point is that you can follow your joy, even if intermittently, for a few moments a day, week or whatever.

I learned something else during those years. If at all possible, find love and joy in what you're doing.

That was easy for me; I was raising two captivating youngsters. They were just the opposite in nature, so there was never a dull moment. I honestly believed, at the time, and I still believe that there is nothing more creative than raising children. Today, I look at them as adults and realize how well their God-given talents and characteristics have shaped and influenced who they are. I would have it no other way. They are my joy forever.

Years ago I counseled Ellen, a woman in her late forties who was still grieving the loss of her first love. She wept a great deal while relating her story. Her mother died when she was young. To help her through her grief, a concerned aunt paid a well known dance studio so that Ellen could take lessons. When in her teens, she fell in love with a young ballet enthusiast whom she met in one of the studio classes. They not only danced together as a team, they had dreams of eventually marrying.

However, her domineering father saw no future in their plans, broke up the relationship and forced her into a marriage with an older, well-to-do businessman. Heartbroken, Ellen never danced again. The young man became well-known in ballet, eventually married and had a family.

When I first met Ellen, she was almost penniless. Her husband had been good to her, she said, but he had died several years previously leaving most of his money and property to his children by another marriage. She never had worked and was living off the sale of a house he had left her. She told me that she only wanted to know and to do God's will.

Perhaps she just needed someone to talk and pray with because when I asked her what talents she had other than painting, she said that she loved playing the piano and singing. In fact, at one time she had taken lessons in piano, organ and voice. Because the young teen-aged dancer had not shared her interest in playing instruments and singing, she was not torn apart by memories of his being connected with music in that way.

Her countenance brightened when our prayers were answered and she found professional work. First she played organ in a church, then was hired to play piano and sing in a fashionable restaurant. She had found her joy, something all her own that was not subject to anyone else telling her what to do or even being with her.

She also discovered that when one plan does not go the way she thinks it will, there is always another fascinating challenge to pursue that will be just as creative and rewarding. It was all, she decided, in finding what she loved to do and doing it because that was God's plan for her life.

"Commit to the Lord whatever you do, and your plans will succeed" (Proverbs 16:3).

Loving and Serving

Toward the completion of the eidetic process each of my students discovers that he needs to discipline himself to stop looking within himself every moment for fulfillment. I urge you also, my Friend, to understand that your reason for living is within *and* all around you. For some who have spent a lifetime striving to become more God-like, this might be a difficult concept to accept at first glance. Perhaps you have been taught that God is found only during the inner Silence. Perhaps you have discounted anything that is material or "of the world" and on some level of consciousness have perceived the physical body as fundamentally base and prone to evil.

With your present awareness, however, there is no longer any logic—especially Divine Logic—in such thinking. Now, your perception is more God-like and you know that your body is sacred and Good in His sight. You have been molded from the beginning by the activity of God's Spirit and you know that Love and Truth are all encompassing. I mean to say that God created in Love and that all God created is truly Good. Your body is the Temple of the Living God. It is the way you regard, care for and express love through your body that determines its effectiveness and its value.

You are wiser now and you are learning a new and wondrous thing: Divine Logic is not only for God's use, it is for *you* to use as your very own. Much of what you have viewed as magical, coincidental or perhaps miraculous, you now view with unveiled eyes. You are finding that when you use Principle, you are no longer controlled by destructive, "evil" forces.

Before your present understanding, you seldom recognized the constant activity of Spirit in your life. When in the middle of a difficult situation, your mind was too occupied with worry to perceive anything good. But you have observed, recently, that what seems to be a tragedy while it is happening, later shows itself to be a blessing. Now you see the Truth that everything contains a blessing, that everything is always in Divine Order. You know that only Good can come and with this knowing, you accept your true heritage as the son or daughter of the Most High.

The following words of Paramahansa Yogananda
speak volumes: "Last night I saw the Christ. I beheld
his face; and just as he passed out of my vision I perceived also the delusive evil force manifest as Satan.
It was a strangely awesome experience—those two
universal forces passed through my body: one of them
as the infinite joy and peace of God, the other as the
great outgoing power of Cosmic Delusion. That sa-
tanic force could not harm me, only try to frighten
me. In exalted states of consciousness experienced
as one goes toward Spirit, those two forces are beheld distinctly as the essential duality of manifested
creation; but in the highest *samadhi* I see there is
naught but Spirit, the Unmanifested Absolute. On
the relative plane, however, one sees at work in the
cosmos the power of evil and the power of Christ
Consciousness, the power of Satan and the power of
God." (4)

Serving Without Efforting

After learning to love the Christ Truth in yourself, what could possibly be your next step but to seek
the Christ in all others? Wherever you find that Love
and Truth are missing, you yearn to do everything
you can to facilitate the expression of these God-given
qualities. I emphasize *facilitate* the expression of God.
That is, do not force your own thoughts and ideas of
how these qualities are to express in anyone, including yourself. Notice, Friend, that when you put forth
a lot of personal effort, you probably are expecting
something in return and Spirit is *not* moving *freely*
through you.

Have you ever thought, "I've done so much for

her, and she's given me nothing in return"? Sure, it's great to do for others and when you do something for someone with no expectation of return, you really are doing what Jesus' life teaches. You find that Spirit is free to inspire your attitudes and actions and *you* are free to understand the deep needs of your friend.

The Old Testament advice is: "Whatever your hand finds to do, do it with all your might" (Ecclesiastes 9:10). Perhaps this has had a lot to do with the work ethic that has driven citizens of our country from the moment the Pilgrims landed on Plymouth Rock. But that was then. Now we want more leisure time to be creative and to be with friends and family.

The twentieth century included the Agricultural Era, the Industrial Revolution and, besides other devastating trauma, the Great Depression which was sandwiched between two World Wars. Our society is now entrenched in a high-paced Technological Era. We are finding that the discoveries and inventions we expected would give us freedom from labor are actually increasing the pace of living and that people are "needing" more and more things. Thus for supply to keep up with demand, priority still is given to long, hard hours of work—mental though it often is—to fulfill those "needs." Consequently, happiness is mistakenly thought to be found in money, power and possessions.

Wouldn't you think we could take the Bible to heart more than we do? Jesus tells us, in Matthew 6:28, to consider the lilies of the field; they do not labor as we do, yet are dressed in great splendor. We read, but we have not learned the teaching in Matthew 6:31-33: "So do not worry, saying, 'What shall we eat?' or 'What shall we drink?' or 'What shall we wear?' For the pagans run after all these things, and your heavenly Father knows that you need them. But seek first his kingdom and his righteousness, and all these things will be given to you as well."

Why is it that our Christian society cannot take these words more seriously, even more literally? We may not always succeed, but the less we worry about our needs and deeds, the better. Doctors and psychologists agree that worry and stress go together in causing physical illness. It appears that many simply do not believe the words in Matthew 6, so they throw away the Truth of God and fill their minds with worry and their bodies with poor health.

Jon Kabat-Zinn, in *Wherever You Go, There You Are,* explains his understanding of this mystical, seemingly contradictory Principle clearly. "Non-doing can arise within action as well as in stillness. The inward stillness of the doer merges with the outward activity to such an extent that the action does itself. Effortless activity. Nothing is forced. There is no exertion of the will, no small-minded "I," "me," or "mine" to lay claim to a result, yet nothing is left undone. Non-doing is a cornerstone of mastery in any realm of activity." (5)

What do you do and how do you do it, my Friend? In Mark 3:35, Jesus called everyone who does God's will, His brother and sister and mother. Moreover, He quoted and approved the Old Testament statement in Psalm 82:6 that we are gods (John 10:34).

Since you are a god, dearly Beloved, you have open communion with your Creator for whom nothing is impossible. Surely you understand that when you do nothing unless the Father does it through you, there is no stress necessary. You see, when you practice the Presence, the work you do is effortless activity, or as a cherished minister-friend of mine says, your work is done "without efforting."

Take heed, dearly Beloved, for this can be a sign. When you find yourself putting forth great effort to accomplish something on your own, you are doing it for your personal glory, not for God's. Oh, perhaps not consciously so, but there is some erroneous attitude in your subconscious driving you. It tries to get its way by acting out, and all the while your soul is crying for spiritual healing. When you allow Spirit to move through you, transforming your humanness into perfect Oneness with your Creator, you will perceive with God's eyes. You will believe His Word, love with His Love and live according to His Truth.

In the beautiful words of Meister Eckhart, "A perfect person will be so cleared of self, so wrapped in God, so obedient to His willing, that his joy will be in the escape from himself and from mortal concerns, and in consciousness of nothing but Divinity . . . He wants only what God wants, and wants it God's way." (6)

And now, Beloved Friend, in fulfilling the guidance I have received from Our Father-Mother-Creator, I toss this bread onto the universal waters. God's peace remains with me because I know that wherever I am, God is; wherever you are, God is. And so it is that all is well.

Thank You, Father-Mother-Creator, that this is so.

Preparation for Meditation

In preparation for the coming meditation, find a comfortable position. Stretch your body and get ready to stretch your mental and emotional faculties, so you can freely contemplate the noo-sphere. This word refers to the sphere of human consciousness and mental activity, especially in regard to its influence on living beings, their environment and evolution.

To break through this noo-sphere to a higher realm of awareness and activity, a transformation of global thinking and feeling is necessary. That will be achieved when enough individuals are mentally wholesome and emotionally peaceful. When the mind and heart are pure, there is righteousness in actions. This means that men and women freely choose to act according to God's will right here on earth. One benefit of being free in this way is that we each will be communicating with the Christ Spirit in others. Together, we will transform the world, starting with its understanding of our relationship to God, the Source of all that is.

There is a cosmic balancing act occurring in the noo-sphere where psychic power struggles reflect the world-wide atrocities that humans commit against one another. This is a new millennium, and we are learning a new thing. We are coming together in new ways. For instance, the *roles* of men and women are no longer as split and diametrically opposed as they once were. Now we are closer to Truth and can be more honest with each other. When Love and Truth are accepted, rapid and wonderful changes take place on the core level of the persons involved.

Indeed, relationships are changing today. In the

new world, women join the work force if they want and men can choose—without diminishing their self-esteem—to remain home caring for the children. Distance is separating countries less and less. With the advent of television and the internet, isolation is virtually impossible. Humanity's violence against humanity is no longer hidden. It is being brought to the fore and corrected by those with less rigid, more compassionate beliefs and customs in which the rights of all humans are accepted and honored.

One day we will have learned to love enough to distribute the earth's bounty equally, to use and to share scientific and technical advances for the good of all. Hungry, war-like countries eventually will yield to Love and Truth because their basic material needs for food, shelter and security will be met. They will be aware of their spiritual hunger and allow it to be nourished by others' demonstration of God's Love and Wisdom.

But to support them through this transformation, our demonstration of Love and Wisdom must be unconditional and unfailing. This means that *we* need to grow spiritually in both the masculine and feminine aspects of consciousness. When my students near the completion of Eidetic Therapy, they find that their thinking and feeling natures have come together in harmonious agreement. So much so that determining what is a thought and what is a feeling is almost impossible. As the within, so the without. Thus looking into another's soul, there is no separation. We perceive neither male nor female. Can it be that the line between the yin and yang is being dissolved into its native nothingness? Let us look again at *The Gospel According To Thomas:*

Jesus said to them:

When you make the two one, and

When you make the inner as the outer
and the outer as the inner and the above as
the below and when you make the male and
the female into a single one, so that the
male will not be male and the female (not)
be female . . . then shall you enter {the King-
dom}. (7)

Log. 22; 24-30; 34

An Eidetic Vision: The Manifestation of Heaven on Earth

Now, if you will, dearly Beloved, prepare for your meditation.

Sit back, close your eyes and enter your Christed Self. Your Life Essence surrounds and enfolds you. Here, you feel the Most Ancient One closer than ever before, closer than anything in the world.

Whatever Divine Desire you decree will be established for you. You are here to decree peace on earth. Your family and friends are with you. Join hands with them. Include in your circle everyone you know and love.

Looming all around is a veil of global consciousness. You are accustomed to this shadowy veil. It is the noo-sphere. It is separating Heaven and earth.

Your circle of loved ones sing songs of Truth and Love, songs of Global Peace. When ready, link arms with all the people of the world. Keep singing. Sing until everyone acknowledges sacred universal Truth. Sing until everyone is filled with divine Love. Your

Father-Mother-God is nourishing all of creation. You are caressed in her womb-like Presence.

Enfolded and protected in this mystical aura of Truth and Love, all children of God are mother, father, sister and brother to one another. There is no difference racially, sexually or intellectually. Look into the others' souls and you will see that this is so. Remember, "many who are first will be last, and many who are last will be first" (Matthew 19:30). First or last is of no consequence.

Hand in hand, arm in arm, you move, perhaps float—let it be however your vision unfolds. You advance through the veil of human consciousness toward the splendor of a new sphere of knowing and being. All together, now, you enter the Kingdom of God right here on earth. Global consciousness has been transformed.

Let this experience of God and the Kingdom develop as it will. Without efforting, stay in the Kingdom. Rest there. Know that the splendor of your vision, your blessed ability to receive it, and the power you hold to achieve it, all belong to God.

Your will be done. Your will be done, dear Lord.

Thank You, God, that this is so. We pray in and through the nature of Jesus, the Christed One. Thank You, Father-Mother-Creator. Amen.

Epilogue

The first draft of *Revisiting the Garden and Deciding to Stay* was in my publisher's hands by early August, 2001. This epilogue was written during the weeks following September 11, 2001.

The twin towers have fallen. Through shock and tears we wonder why. We watch the same TV images again and again: the devastating attack, fire and smoke and people jumping from windows. Firemen clear away debris to save a few out of thousands—to find even one. Policemen, clergymen, loved ones demonstrate selfless bravery and compassion. Nations the world over express condolences and support. Days become weeks but the heaviness does not go. We slow down. We must *do* something. What *can* we do? We humble ourselves before our Creator. Hindu, Muslim and Christian clergy unite, leading services; we all pray to One God. A new consciousness is blossoming: When one person or group of persons is wounded, the wound harms everyone all over the earth but it also draws us together for healing. We are not perfect yet and towers are not the most enduring thing.

With heavy heart we defend ourselves and attempt to heal bodies and to nourish souls. An Afghani toddler clutches a yellow food bag, empty now, as empty as his mother's withered breast. Amthrax. The fear of nuclear war. What are we to do? Love our enemies? But what are we to do with our anger? We remember other wars: Vietnam, Korea, World War ll—the atom bomb! We look at our own crimes against others: our early atrocities against American Indians, our inhumanity in bringing Africans here as slaves, our arrogance and self-righteousness throughout recent history that surely—somehow—has contributed to the demoralization of the Third World countries. Lord, forgive us our trespasses as we forgive those who trespass against us. As well as we were able, we fought a good fight. But we are changing. We acknowledge the fact that we are evolving from the survival of the fittest consciousness into a new awareness of one another. We are growing spiritually. In Truth we are all One Spirit. An eye for an eye is no longer the answer. The time has come to stop crucifying the Truth in one another.

Why have our towers fallen? It is not ours to *rationalize* ourselves out of this mystery. We cannot. However, it is ours to love God and to love our neighbor—even if he is our enemy—as much as we love ourselves. It is ours to thank God for the grace bestowed upon us with which we rise from the ashes of nuclear explosions, gas chambers, starvation camps and fallen towers. We are made in the Image-Likeness. It is ours to claim our heritage, to hold the vision of peace and love for everyone all over the world.

It is ours to watch the Father working through us to establish His Kingdom on earth. God bless us all.

Bibliography

Preface

(1) Ahsen, Akhter.
Excerpt from *Manhunt In The Desert: the epic dimensions of man.* Copyright (c) 1979 by Akhter Ahsen, Ph.D. New York, New York: Brandon House, Inc. Reprinted by permission of Akhter Ahsen, Ph.D.

Prologue

(1) Ahsen, Akhter.
Psycheye: Self-Analytic Consciousness; page 14. Copyright (c) 1977 by Akhter Ahsen, Ph.D. New York, New York: Brandon House, Inc. Reprinted by permission of Akhter Ahsen, Ph.D.

Chapter 1: The Movement of Spirit

(1) Warren, Greg.
Eidetic Poem from *Revisiting the Garden And Deciding to Stay*. Copyright (c) 2001 by Dana J. Voght. Philadelphia, Pennsylvania: Xlibris Publishing Corp. Reprinted by permission of Greg Warren.

(2) Warren, Greg.
Letter excerpt from *Revisiting the Garden And Deciding to Stay*. Copyright (c) 2001 by Dana J. Voght Philadelphia, Pennsylvania: Xlibris Publishing Corp. Reprinted by permission of Greg Warren.

Chapter 2: Awakening to the Activity of Spirit

(1) O'Donohue, John.
Excerpt from *Anam Cara: A Book of Celtic Wisdom* by John O'Donohue. Copyright (c) 1997 by John O'Donohue. Reprinted by permission of HarperCollins Publishers, Inc.

(2) Radin, Dean.
"Moving Mind Moving Matter" Article by Dean Radin, psi researcher. *Noetic Science Review*, Summer 1998, page 22. Reprinted by permission of The Institute of Noetic Sciences. Petaluma, California: Institute of Noetic Sciences.

(3) Freeman, James Dillet.
"The Prayer of Protection" Poem by James Dillet Freeman, Unity Minister.Reprinted by permission of Unity School of Christianity Unity Village, Missouri.

(4) *The Gospel According to Thomas.*
Excerpted pages 17,19. Established and translated by A. Guillaumont, H.-Ch. Puech, G.

Quispel, W. Till, and Yassah Abd Al Masih. Copyright (c) E. J. Brill 1959. New York and Evanston: Harper and Row. Reprinted by permission of Brill Academic Publishers, PO Box 9000; 2300 PA Leiden, the Netherlands.

(5) O'Donohue, John.
Excerpt from *Anam Cara: A Book of Celtic Wisdom* by John O'Donohue. Copyright (c) 1997 by John O'Donohue. Reprinted by permission of HarperCollins Publishers, Inc.

Chapter 3: The Choice Is Yours—or Is It?

(1) Freeman, James Dillet.
"The Prayer of Protection" Poem by James Dillet Freeman, Unity Minister. Reprinted by permission of Unity School of Christianity, Unity Village, Missouri.

(2) Wallechinsky, David.
"He Killed My Daughter, But I Don't Want Him To Die" Article by David Wallechinsky. *The Parade Magazine,* January 18, 1998, page 5, insert of *The Stuart News.* Reprinted by permission of *The Stuart News,* Stuart, Florida

(3) Long, Max Freedom.
The Secret Science At Work, page 113. Copyright (c) 1953 by Max Freedom Long. Marina del Rey, California: DeVorss Publications. Reprinted by permission of DeVorss & Company, Publisher.

(4) Ahsen, Akhter.
Psycheye: Self Analytic Consciousness, page 52. Copyright (c) 1977 by Akhter Ahsen, Ph.D. New York,

New York: Brandon House, Inc.Reprinted by permission of Akhter Ahsen, Ph.D.

(5) Anderson, Terry.
"Small Graces" Article by Terry Anderson. *Guideposts* magazine, September 1993, page 2. Copyright (c) 1993 by Guideposts, Carmel, New York 10512. Reprinted with permission of Guideposts.

Chapter 4: The Measure of Your Self-Esteem

(1) Fillmore, Charles (1854-1948).
Mysteries of Genesis, page 45. By Charles Fillmore, co-founder of Unity School of Christianity. Reprinted by permission of Unity Books, Unity School of Christianity, Unity Village, Missouri.

(2) Fillmore, Charles.
Talks on Truth, page 130. By Charles Fillmore, co-founder of Unity School of Christianity. Reprinted by permission of Unity Books, Unity School of Christianity, Unity Village, Missouri.

(3) Ahsen, Akhter.
Psycheye: Self Analytic Consciousness, page 44. Copyright (c) 1977 by Akhter Ahsen Ph.D. New York, New York: Brandon House, Inc. Reprinted by permission of Akhter Ahsen, Ph.D.

(4) Fillmore, Charles.
Mysteries of Genesis, page 45. By Charles Fillmore, co-founder of Unity School of Christianity, Reprinted by permission of Unity Books Unity School of Christianity Unity Village, Missouri

Chapter 5: Do You Really Want to Forgive?

(1) Jampolsky, Gerald G.

Love Is Letting Go Of Fear, page 65. Excerpt from *Love Is Letting Go Of Fear*. Copyright (c) 1979 by Gerald G. Jampolsky, M.D. and Jack O. Keeler. Reprinted by permission of Celestial Arts, PO Box 7123, Berkeley, California 94707.

(2) Wilson, Ernest C. (1896-1982).

Quotation of Ernest C. Wilson, Unity Minister. Source: notes of Dana J. Voght, Unity Minister.

(3) Gandhi, Mahatma. (1869-1948).

Gandhi: All Men Are Brothers, page 99. Compiled and edited by Krishna Kripalani. Copyright (c) 1980 by The Continuum Publishing Corp. New York, New York: The Continuum Publishing Corp. Reprinted by permission of The Continuum Publishing Corp.

(4) Kern, Jack D.

An Experiment In Love. Pamphlet by Jack D. Kern, Unity Minister. Published by the Assn. of Unity Churches, Lee's Summit, Missouri. Reprinted by permission of Jack D. Kern.

(5) ten Boom, Corrie (1892-1983).

"I'm Still Learning to Forgive" Article by Corrie ten Boom. Excerpted with permission by *Guideposts* magazine. Copyright (c) 1972 by Guideposts, Carmel, New York 10512. All rights reserved.

Chapter 6: The Story of Ruth I

(1) Herzog Jr., Arthur & Holiday, Billie.
God Bless The Child - Arthur Herzog, Jr., Billie
Holiday. Copyright (c) 1941 - Edward B. Marks
Music Company. Copyright renewed. Used by
permission. All rights renewed.

(2) Ahsen, Akhter.
Psycheye: Self-Analytic Consciousness, page 75. Copyright (c) 1977 by Akhter Ahsen, Ph.D. New York,
New York: Brandon House, Inc. Reprinted by
permission of Akhter Ahsen, Ph.D.

Chapter 7: The Story of Ruth II

(1) Ahsen, Akhter.
Psycheye: Self-Analytic Consciousness, page 175.
Copyright (c) 1977 by Akhter Ahsen, Ph.D. New
York, New York: Brandon House, Inc. Reprinted
by permission of Akhter Ahsen, Ph.D.

Chapter 8: To Stay or Not to Stay

(1) Jampolsky, Gerald G.
Teach Only Love. Copyright (c) 2000 by Gerald
G. Jampolsky, M.D. From the book, *Teach Only
Love.* Beyond Words Publishing, Hillsboro, Or-
egon.

(2) Lazarus, Emma (1849-1887).
"The New Colossus." Poem by Emma Lazarus.
Appears on the pedestal of the Statue of Lib-
erty. Written in 1883. Now in public domain.

Chapter 9: Deciding to Stay

(1) Ahsen, Akhter.
Psycheye: Self-Analytic Consciousness, page 44. Copyright (c) 1977 by Akhter Ahsen, Ph.D. New York, New York: Brandon House, Inc. Reprinted by permission of Akhter Ahsen, Ph.D.

Chapter 10: For His Greater Glory

(1) Yogananda, Paramahansa (1893-1952).
"Applied Spiritual Science" Article by Paramahansa Yogananda. *Self-Realization* Magazine, Winter 2000, page 41. Published by Self-Realization Fellowship. Los Angeles, California.
(2) Fillmore, Charles.
Keep a True Lent, page 58. By Charles Fillmore, co-founder of Unity School of Christianity. Reprinted by permission of Unity Books, Unity School of Christianity. Unity Village, Missouri.
(3)Ahsen, Akhter (1260-1327).
Excerpt from *Manhunt In The Desert: the epic dimensions of man.* Copyright (c) 1979 by Akhter Ahsen, Ph.D. New York, New York: Brandon House, Inc. Reprinted by permission of Akhter Ahsen, Ph.D.
(4) Yogananda, Paramahansa.
"The Spiritual Celebration of Christmas" Article by Paramahansa Yogananda. *Self-Realization* Magazine, Winter 2000, page 7. Published by Self-Realization Fellowship. Los Angeles, California.
(5) Kabat-Zinn, Jon.
Wherever You Go, There You Are, page 40. Copy-

right (c) 1994 by Jon Kabat-Zinn. New York, New York: Hyperion.

(6) Eckhart, Meister (1260-1327).
Meister Eckhart. Quotation in *Self-Realization* Magazine, Winter 2000, page 17. Published by Self Realization Fellowship. Los Angeles, California.

(7) *The Gospel According To Thomas,* pages 17, 19.
Translated by A. Guillaumont, H.-Ch.Puech, G. Quispel, W. Till and Yassah Abd Al Masih. Harper & Row, 1959. Reprinted by permission of Brill Academic Publishers. PO Box 9000, 2300 PA Leiden, The Netherlands.

Suggested Reading

Ahsen, Akhter. *Ganesh*. New York, New York: Brandon House, Inc., 1995.

Because modern analysis is devoid of Spirit, life itself is disfigured and the future is insecure. The material in *Ganesh* atones for this damage.

The commentary on consciousness in this book resonates with material from the Vedas and other sacred literature. The intriguing figure of Ganesh is the central reference point in consciousness that leads to other godly figures revealing various concerns regarding our thinking and feeling habits and attitudes.

Ahsen, Akhter. *Manhunt in the Desert: the epic dimensions of man*. New York, New York: Brandon House, Inc., 1979.

Manhunt in the Desert is an epic poem of confrontation between the invincible Sahara and the invincible man. What it means to you and how you are going to use these activating symbols are the secrets told in this highly contemporary book on transformation of consciousness.

The reader is led into self-examination and is presented with the realization that each one of us is traveling in his own lonesome desert. Still no one is alone, because the quest for water rather than sand is shared by all. And the quest is fulfilled as the traveler finds one liberating reality after another, finally revealing that the eternal waters have been within himself and within everyone else all along.

Ahsen, Akhter. *Psycheye.* New York, New York: Brandon House, Inc., 1977.

Psycheye is internationally recognized as a leading book of self-healing exercises. Calling attention to the forces of growth within each individual, it emphasizes the freedom of everyone to decide to restructure his/her emotional life.

The process detailed in *Psycheye* involves the individual in spontaneous imagery of life experiences in such a way that it heals unpleasant memories and guides the participant into a more fulfilling life.

Daya Mata, Sri. *Only Love.* Self Realization Fellowship, 1976. Los Angeles, California.

This book is an enlightened guide for all who are searching for closer human relationships and for more constant communication with God.

The reader of *Only Love* learns new, effective methods of expressing love and compassion in the complexity of today's changing world.

Fillmore, Charles (1854-1948). *Keep a True Lent.* Unity Village, Missouri: Unity Books.

This book is a guide for the forty day period of Lenten prayer and fasting, followed by the resurrection on Easter Sunday. The emphasis is on the metaphysical experience of fasting: abstaining from all unworthy thoughts and feasting upon the Good and the True. With an expanded consciousness, the individual is resurrected into closer communion with God.

An inspiring message, a suggested Bible reading and a meaningful meditation for each day are included, guiding the reader into a finer, closer awareness of Spirit.

Fillmore, Charles. *The Twelve Powers of Man.* Unity Village, Missouri: Unity books.

This book is a brilliant metaphysical explanation of the twelve powerful faculties within men and women.

When these mental faculties are used according to Principle, they increase the individual's material manifestations as well as his/her spiritual growth.

Fillmore, Myrtle (1845-1931). *Myrtle Fillmore's Healing Letters.* Unity Village, Missouri: Unity Books.

These extracts from the letters of Myrtle Page Fillmore, Mother of Unity, blessed all to whom they were sent. Today they continue to bless all who read this book. Love and wisdom, health of mind and body, happiness and success are everyone's divine heritage.

Fillmore, Myrtle. *How to Let God Help You.* Unity Village, Missouri. Unity Books.

Myrtle Fillmore was—and still is, in Spirit—a counselor and teacher to those who want to learn the

Truth of Jesus Christ. In this book she speaks as a friend to each reader.

Material used in *How to Let God Help You* comes from Myrtle Fillmore's letters, from her hand written spiritual notes and from the basic Principles of Truth in her lectures. In gentle, loving—yet strong—words, she inspires and uplifts her readers, just as she did during her life on earth.

Moore, Thomas. *Care of the Soul.* New York, New York, HarperCollins Publishers.

Care of the Soul, by this beautifully perceptive author, illuminates the reader's awareness of reality. We have much to learn and to receive by reclaiming our individual souls.

All states of being—even depression—hold messages of Light that heal, uplift and transform. Reclaiming one's soul makes one sensitive to these messages, to the souls in others and to the beauty in other cultures. By listening to the sacred messages of the soul, we touch the global soul and thus global peace can be established.

Smith, Hannah Whitall (1832-1911). *The Christian's Secret to a Happy Life.* Grand Rapids, Michigan: Fleming H. Revel.

This inspired classic is written for those who seek practical rather than theological guidance. The reader's attitudes, actions and motivations are examined in the light of those who walk and talk with God.

A Quaker, rebel and realist, the author took her Bible promises seriously. She tested them and found them to be true. In this book she reveals her secret:

how to obtain peace and confidence, success and security for every day of your life.

Yogananda, Paramahansa (1893-1952). *Autobiography of a Yogi*. Self-Realization Fellowship. 1977. Los Angeles, California.

Autobiography of a Yogi opens the reader's eyes to an awareness of Ultimate Reality that is rarely experienced in western culture. Reading this book presents possibilities for humankind to manifest every good desire and to contribute to peace in everyday life and throughout the world.

Yogananda, Paramahansa. *The Science of Religion*. Self-Realization Fellowship. 1974. Los Angeles, California.

To experience the most intimate connection with God, one must be receptive to Him every moment.

To be too busy for God, not to perceive His hand in every aspect of life is to be not really alive. The reader of this classic discovers that there is no separation between true science and spirituality.

Yogananda, Paramahansa. *Whispers From Eternity*. Self-Realization Fellowship. 1973. Los Angeles, California.

This book is written for all who yearn for God, no matter what the religious background or faith has been. Beautifully poetic meditations, prayers and invocations to the Lord speak to the Cosmic Heart and all become One.

Printed in the United States
6225